THE BIBLE
IN THE
TWELFTH CENTURY

THE BIBLE
IN THE
TWELFTH CENTURY

An Exhibition of Manuscripts
at the Houghton Library
by Laura Light

THE HARVARD COLLEGE LIBRARY

CAMBRIDGE, MASSACHUSETTS

1988

DESIGN: *Larry Webster*
PHOTOGRAPHY: *Rick Stafford, Fogg Art Museum*
COMPOSITION AND PRINTING: *Thomas Todd Company, Boston*
BINDING: *Bay State Bindery, Boston*

Contents

Introduction

A MANUSCRIPT WRITTEN in the twelfth century, probably in the Augustinian priory of Llanthony in Monmouth, MS Typ 194 of the Houghton Library, contains a remarkable story about a vellum Bible. Part of a collection of great antiquity, *De Vitis Patrum*, the story, entitled "Patience," may have been read to the brothers during meals. It is a brief but highly condensed narrative, and I would like to offer it as an introduction to this catalogue.

> The brothers told of Abbot Gelasius who had a vellum manuscript worth 18 soldi. It contained both the Old and the New Testaments entire; and he placed it in the church so that any of the brothers who wished might read from it. Now it happened that an itinerant brother visited the Elder and seeing the codex he desired it, seized it, and removed it and left. The Elder, however, although he had seen this happen, did not follow to arrest the thief.
>
> The thief went to town to determine to whom he might sell the manuscript. And when he had found one willing to buy, he forthwith offered it at a price of 16 soldi. The buyer, wishing to test the price said "First give me the manuscript so that I might ascertain whether I should pay so much." Therefore the thief gave it to him on approval. When the buyer received the manuscript he took it to Abbot Gelasius to see if it was a good codex and worth the price; and he told him what the seller was asking. The Elder said "Buy it. It is a good codex and worth the price he told you."
>
> However the buyer returned to the thief and did not repeat what the Elder had told him. Rather he said "Look, I showed it to Abbot Gelasius, and he told me it was too expensive and not worth what you are asking." When the seller heard this he said "Did not the Elder say anything else?" and the other answered "Nothing." "Well then," said the thief, "I do not want to sell this codex."
>
> Full of regret he went to the Elder to seek penance, and he asked him to take back the manuscript. The Elder refused. But the brother said, "If you do not take it back I shall never be saved." And the Elder replied "If you cannot be saved unless I take it back, then take it back I will." And the brother remained with him until his death, growing from the example of the old man's patience.

The subject is patience. Gelasius was a patient man, and his behavior is offered as a model. The narrative technique, however, is one of a continuous disruption of the listener's expectations through the peculiar actions of the three actors. There is surprise upon surprise, the greatest one being the buyer's unsuccessful attempt at distorting the Abbot's disinterestedness. Gelasius's message gets through, and the thief is touched and saved. It is apparently a story about God's patience and an example of the complexity of certain simple old narratives. It is also a story about a Bible.

Two things we would like to learn from this narrative are the cost of the Bible in the Middle Ages and the availability of the Bible to readers. Despite its inclusion in a twelfth-century manuscript, the great antiquity of the collection *De Vitis Patrum*, which was translated from Greek into Latin in the early years of the church, rules it out as a source of knowledge of the twelfth century. The introduction by the compiler of this catalogue will suggest that Bibles as such were in scarce supply even though knowledge of scripture permeated the culture. The value of a *soldus*, silver or gold, at the time this Bible was having its adventures is unknown, at least to this writer.

What remains astonishingly constant is the great value of vellum manuscripts through the ages and the behavior patterns of those who move them from place to place. Despite the characters' otherwise surprising behavior, the mark-down of price for the stolen manuscript, the acceptance "on approval" by the buyer, even the reduction of the official estimate have a lively and timeless ring. Graham Pollard has said that old manuscripts are like old houses, constructed and altered, defaced, embellished, and even moved around by teams of largely anonymous individuals. The manuscripts being displayed in the present exhibition all have their histories as well, and one of the tasks of the cataloguer of medieval manuscripts is to uncover those histories, discover provenance and reveal manipulation, in the service both of text and of the artifact itself.

To these ends the Library has at last embarked on an ambitious program of cataloguing all of its Medieval and Renaissance manuscripts according to modern scholarly standards. After having been initiated by the Library, this program is now being supported by a grant from The National Endowment for the Humanities. The central individual in this program, assisted by a number of specialists, is the cataloguer Laura Light, now well-embarked on describing between 1300 and 1400 objects of considerable complexity. This exhibition on the Bible in the twelfth century, organized by Ms. Light, and this catalogue, which she has compiled, are by-products of this activity, intended not merely to inform and give pleasure, but also to announce abroad that the Harvard Library intends to do justice to these important holdings.

The main individual entries given here begin with descriptions, intended to be useful to specialists, of the manuscripts' physical characteristics. Each of these descriptions is followed by remarks for a more general readership about the type of manuscript shown. The concluding checklist of the Library's other twelfth-century manuscripts is tentative and preliminary, and I have responsibility for that myself.

Aside from what we owe to the National Endowment for the Humanities, I should like to acknowledge our debt and express all of our warmest gratitude to those friends who helped finance this enterprise: William Bentinck-Smith, W. H. Bond, The Department of Classics, Helmut N. Friedlaender, John Heller, Susan M.

Hilles, The Hunt Foundation, The Richard and Natalie Jacoff Foundation, James M. Storey, Mr. and Mrs. Paul Van Buren, Mr. and Mrs. Arthur Vershbow, and James E. Walsh.

I should also like to point out here that a great many of the manuscripts described and listed are from the Department of Printing and Graphic Arts, a circumstance that underlines my own long-standing and ongoing debt to Miss Eleanor M. Garvey, Philip Hofer Curator of that Department, the generosity and openness of whose collaboration have, for years, made all the difference.

Rodney G. Dennis
Curator of Manuscripts

Abbreviations of Works Frequently Cited

CC: Corpus christianorum

CPL: E. Dekkers and A. Gaar, eds., *Clavis patrum latinorum*. Sacris erudiri 3 (Steenbrugge, 2nd. ed. 1961)

De Hamel, *Glossed Books*: C. F. R. de Hamel, *Glossed Books of the Bible and the Origins of the Paris Booktrade* (Woodbridge, Suffolk 1984)

De Ricci: S. De Ricci, with the assistance of W. J. Wilson, *Census of Medieval and Renaissance Manuscripts in the United States and Canada* (New York 1935 and 1937; index 1940)

Faye and Bond: C. U. Faye and W. H. Bond, *Supplement to the Census of Medieval and Renaissance Manuscripts in the United States and Canada* (New York 1962)

Harvard Cat. **(1955):** Harvard College Library, *Illuminated and Calligraphic Manuscripts* (Cambridge, Mass. 1955)

Leclercq, "Manuscrits cisterciens": Jean Leclercq, O.S.B., "Textes et manuscrits cisterciens dans des bibliothèques des Etas-Unis," *Traditio* 17 (1961) 163-183

PL: J. P. Migne, ed., *Patrologia latina*

Smalley, *Study of the Bible*: Beryl Smalley, *The Study of the Bible in the Middle Ages* (Oxford, 3rd. rev. ed. 1983)

Stegmüller: F. Stegmüller, *Repertorium biblicum medii aevi* (Madrid 1950-61), and *Supplementum*, with assistance of N. Reinhardt (Madrid 1976-80)

Wilmart, "La tradition": A. Wilmart, "La tradition des grands ouvrages de Saint Augustin," *Miscellanea Agostiniana. Testi e Studi pubblicati a cura dell'Ordine Eremitano di S. Agostino nel CV centenario dalla morte del Santo Dottore* (Rome 1931) 2:257-315

A List of the Manuscripts Exhibited, with a List of Plates

1. **An introduction to the exhibition;**
   The Morimondo Library Catalogue (fMS Typ 223, f. 227v).
   Plate 1, f. 227v.

I. Case 1. Bibles:

2. fMS Typ 315:
   Initial from a Bible. Northern France (Pontigny?) 1170s (?).
   Plate 2, recto.

3. fMS Typ 119:
   Bible (fragments). Northern France s. XIII³/⁴.

4. MS Typ 3:
   Bible (Genesis-4 Kings). England (?) s. XII^{med-3/4}.
   Plate 3, f. 29.

5. MS Riant 20:
   Gospel Book. Italy s. XII¹.
   Plate 4, ff. 11v-12.

6. MS Lat 264:
   Bible. France (Paris) s. XIII^{med}.

II. Cases 2-3. Liturgical Manuscripts:

7. MS Typ 413:
   Missal and Breviary (fragments). Italy s. XII¹.

8. fMS Typ 210:
   Evangeliary. Italy (Morimondo?) s. XII^{med-3/4} (before 1174/5).
   Plate 5, f. 128v.

9. fMS Typ 138:
   Evangeliary. Italy (Northern?) s. XII^{med-3/4}.

10. fMS Typ 223:
    Office Lectionary. Italy (Morimondo) s. XII^{med-3/4} (before 1174/5).
    Plate 6, f. 49v.

11. MS Typ 444:
    Office Lectionary. Germany (diocese of Trier?) s. XII⁴/⁴ — XIII¹.
    Plate 7, f. 49.

12. fMS Typ 291:
    Sermologus (fragments). Central Italy s. XII^{med}.
    Plate 8, f. 2.

13. fMS Typ 441:
    Homiliary (fragments). Central Italy s. XII^{med}.

14. MS Lat 282:
    Office of the Dead and Hours of the Virgin (fragments).
    Germany s. XII⁴/⁴.
    Plate 9, ff. 26v-27.

III. Cases 4–7. Biblical Commentaries:

15. fMS Typ 703:
    Augustine, Commentary on the Psalms, 101-150.
    Germany (?) s. XII^{med}.
    Plate 10, f. 7.

16. MS Lat 158:
    Remigius of Auxerre, On the Celebration of the Mass.
    Germany s. XII$^{3/4}$.

17. MS Lat 150:
    Augustine, Confessions. Italy (?) s. XII$^{2/4}$.

18. MS Richardson 27:
    Augustine, Confessions. Northern Italy (?) s. XII^{med}.
    Plate 11, f. 19v.

19. fMS Typ 702:
    Gregory, Moralia in Job, books 26-35. Italy (Morimondo) s. XII^2.
    Plate 12, f. 1.

20. MS Lat 167:
    Gregory, Moralia in Job, books 23-29.
    Belgium (Meuse valley) or Germany (?) s. XII$^{3/4}$.
    Plate 13, f. 16v.

21. MS Typ 205:
    Bruno, New Testament Commentary compiled from the works of Gregory.
    Belgium or Germany s. XII$^{med-3/4}$.
    Plate 14, f. 5.

22. MS Richardson 25:
    Gospel Harmony, with the preface by Victor of Capua.
    Belgium (Meuse valley) or Germany (?) s. XII$^{3/4}$.
    Plate 15, f. 6.

23. MS Lat 213:
    Augustine, Commentary on the First Epistle of John.
    Germany (Weissenau?) s. XII^1.

24. MS Richardson 14:
    Augustine, Contra Faustum Manichaeum.
    Northern France (Pontigny?) s. XII^2.
    Plate 16, f. 2.

25. fMS Typ 200:
    Rabanus Maurus, Commentary on Jeremiah and Lamentations.
    Northern France (Pontigny) s. XIII$^{1/4}$.
    Plate 17, f. 86.

26. fMS Typ 202:
    Bede, Commentary on Luke. Germany (Gladbach?) s. XII$^{2/4}$.
    Plate 18, f. 68.

27. fMS Lat 168:
    Jerome, Commentary on Daniel. Central Italy or Tuscany s. XII$^{2/4}$.

28. MS Lat 185:
    Hugh of St. Victor and Bernard of Clairvaux, Monastic Sententiae; and Patristic Extracts. Southern or Central France s. XII².
    Plate 19, f. 41.

29. MS Riant 36:
    Extracts from Patristic Authors and Others.
    Northern France s. XII⁴/⁴; s. XII³/⁴; Germany s. XII².

IV. Cases 8 and 9. Glossed Bibles:

The Ordinary Gloss on the Bible; Introduction.

30. MS Lat 44:
    Priscian, Institutiones grammaticae. France s. XII²/⁴.

31. MS Typ 260:
    Psalms with the Ordinary Gloss. Italy (Tuscany) s. XII².
    Plate 20, ff. 175v-176.

32. fMS Typ 204:
    Leviticus with the Ordinary Gloss. Paris or Germany (?) s. XII^med.
    Plate 21, f. 45.

33. MS Richardson 2:
    Gospel of John with the Ordinary Gloss.
    Italy (Morimondo) s. XII⁴/⁴.
    Plate 22, ff. 47v-48.

34. MS Lat 334:
    Numbers with the Ordinary Gloss. Italy s. XII³/⁴.

35. fMS Typ 29:
    Gilbert de la Porrée, Commentary on the Psalms (77-150).
    Italy (Morimondo) s. XII³/⁴.
    Plate 23, f. 52.

36. MS Typ 277:
    Gilbert de la Porrée, Commentary on the Pauline Epistles.
    Germany s. XII².
    Plate 24, f. 146.

37. fMS Lat 6:
    Sapiential Books with the Ordinary Gloss.
    Northern France or Flanders s. XIII²/⁴.
    Plate 25, f. 77v.

V. Case 10. Texts for the Classroom:

38. MS Lat 226:
    Peter Comestor, Historia scholastica.
    Northern France or Flanders s. XIII^med.

39. fMS Typ 216:
    Peter of Poitiers, Compendium historiae in genealogia christi.
    Northern France s. XIII^in.

A Note on the Contents and Format of the Entries

THE ENTRIES WHICH FOLLOW were written with two main objectives in mind. Above all, it is hoped that they will serve as a very basic introduction to a subject which I find fascinating. Their contents are deliberately miscellaneous, ranging from brief introductions to some of the texts and authors included, to discussions which center on some detail or problem relevant only to the copy of the text exhibited here, such as questions of provenance or date, or some aspect of the material makeup of the manuscript. If these brief discussions tempt someone to explore the field further, they will have successfully fulfilled their intended purpose.

Secondly, it is hoped that this catalogue will help bring the library's twelfth-century manuscripts to the attention of scholars in the field. With this in mind, abbreviated physical descriptions of each item have been included. This exhibition is part of a longer term project of preparing a scholarly catalogue of the library's collections of medieval manuscripts. The descriptions here are by-products of this research, and represent preliminary observations, rather than finished statements. The success of this aspect of the catalogue will be measured by the extent to which it provokes corrections and other comments from the scholarly community.

The contents of the physical descriptions may be summarized briefly as follows: material; the number of leaves, with roman numerals used to designate end leaves; measurements in millimeters, listing the height and width of the book, followed by the height and width of the written space, measured from the top of the minims in the first line, to the feet of the minims in the last; in exceptional cases, measurements of the ruled space are also given, identified as such in the descriptions; instrument and pattern of the ruling; location of prickings, if present; collation; catchwords and signatures; script, with some brief attempt to convey its more important features; and a summary description of decoration. The suggested place of origin and date of the manuscripts are listed in the headings. Due to limitations of space and time, discussion of provenance has been restricted to listing where the library acquired the manuscript, and description of the binding has been omitted; this information can be supplemented in most cases by the previously published descriptions in De Ricci's *Census*, and in the *Supplement* by Faye and Bond. The physical descriptions conclude with second folio references. A bibliography related to the manuscript follows the text of the entry.

The preparation of this catalogue would have been impossible without the encouragement and advice of my friends and colleagues. I owe special thanks to

Carroll Arbogast, Albert Derolez, Paul Meyvaert, Richard Rouse and Roger Stoddard, and even greater thanks to Rodney Dennis for his patient supervision and guidance throughout the project. Their help has improved the entries in many ways; the errors and other defects which may remain are entirely my responsibility.

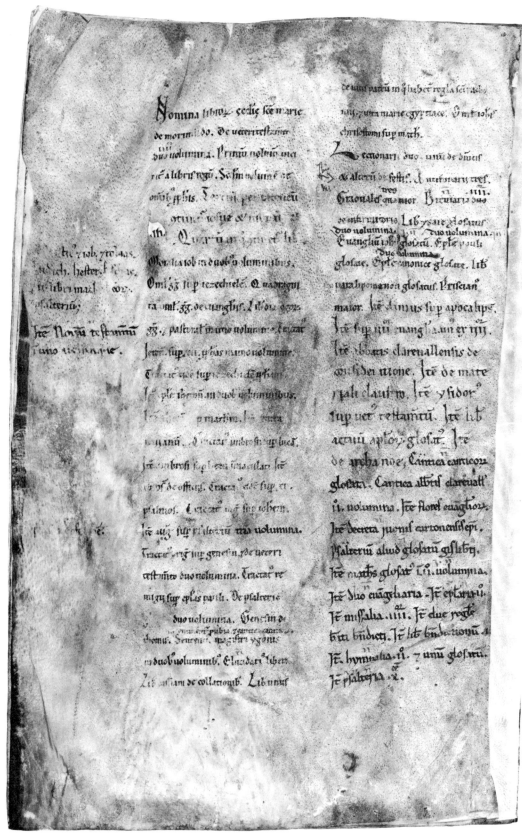

Plate 1. No. 1. fMS Typ 223, f. 227v. 3/5 actual size.

10

1. *An introduction to the exhibition; The Morimondo Library Catalogue*

Italy (Morimondo) s. XII^ex   fMS Typ 223, f. 227v

IN THE LATE TWELFTH CENTURY, an inventory of the books of the Cistercian Abbey of St. Mary at Morimondo in the diocese of Milan in Northern Italy, was written on the verso of the last leaf of an Office Lectionary.[1] This manuscript, now fMS Typ 223 (see cat. no. 10), can be dated before 1174/5 on the basis of liturgical evidence. Morimondo was founded in 1134, and by the second half of the twelfth century it was a flourishing foundation, prosperous enough to begin building a new Church in 1182.[2]

The catalogue was copied in stages. The first writer noted down the titles of about forty volumes. He included only one Bible, a large-format multi-volume Bible, which was evidently still being copied at the time this list was made.[3] The content of most of the books included, however, does center around the Bible, and by far the largest category is biblical commentaries by patristic authors — Gregory the Great's *Moralia in Job*, and his Homilies on Ezechiel and the Gospels, as well as commentaries by Jerome on the Twelve Prophets, Ezechiel and Matthew, by Ambrose on Luke and the Psalms, by Augustine on John and the Psalms, and by Origen on Genesis and the Old Testament, to mention a few examples. Also included are a number of liturgical books, including lectionaries, antiphonaries, graduals and breviaries. The list was completed by two other writers in the late twelfth and early thirteenth centuries, who noted down about twenty more titles. The majority of these are also either biblical commentaries — here a greater proportion are by twelfth-century authors, including a number of copies of books of the Bible with the Ordinary Gloss — or liturgical books.

The history of the dispersal of the collection began during the late fifteenth and early sixteenth centuries, when the historian, Paolo Giovio (1483-1559), acquired a portion of Morimondo's books. The remaining books were catalogued by the Cistercian abbot, F. Ughelli (d. 1670).[4] The remainder of the library was dispersed at the beginning of the nineteenth century, and many of the books purchased by Ulrico Hoepli, and later by J. Martini. Some of the monastery's books remain in Italy, but many were purchased by private collectors, and are now housed in collections in France, England and the United States.[5] In addition to fMS Typ 223, three other twelfth-century manuscripts from Morimondo are included in this exhibition: Gregory's *Moralia*, fMS Typ 702, (see cat. no. 19), the Gospel of John with the Ordinary Gloss, MS Richardson 2 (see cat. no. 33), and Gilbert de la Porrée's Commentary on the Psalms, fMS Typ 29 (see cat. no. 35). A fourth manuscript, a Gospel Lectionary, fMS Typ 210 (see cat. no. 8), is also very likely from

Morimondo. All of these manuscripts, with the exception of fMS Typ 210, are bound in Morimondo's characteristic eighteenth-century bindings of heavy wooden boards covered with undecorated brown leather. They demonstrate that two general styles of script were used at the monastery during the later decades of the twelfth century. fMS Typ 223, and to a lesser extent fMS Typ 210 and fMS Typ 29, are copied in a distinctive type of script, which is sharp and angular in its overall appearance.[6] The first six lines of fMS Typ 702 are copied in a similar script. The scribes who copied the remainder of this manuscript, however, used a much rounder script, as did the scribe of MS Richardson 2.[7]

The books included in this fairly modest list are an excellent introduction to the exhibition as a whole. In particular, the contents of Morimondo's inventory explain why an exhibition devoted to "The Bible in the Twelfth Century" includes only three twelfth-century Bibles (case 1; see cat. nos. 2, 4 and 5). Admittedly, this in part simply reflects the contents of our collection. Practicality, however, is not the only explanation, and the books were chosen to illustrate a point that is too easily overlooked. Any analysis of how the Bible was known and used in the twelfth century must first take into account the fact that relatively few twelfth-century Bibles survive. Twelfth-century Bibles, usually occupying more than one volume, are typically very large and impressive manuscripts, carefully written and often lavishly decorated. An average monastery, like Morimondo, very likely owned only one Bible of this sort. The books included in this exhibition reflect this reality. The Bible was read and studied, to be sure, but the evidence of the surviving books reminds us that our modern conception of reading extensively from a personal copy of the Bible is likely a false one, at least in the majority of cases. As Dom Leclercq has observed, authors such as Saint Bernard of Clairvaux knew the Bible intimately, and cite it profusely in their works. Their citations, however, are often from memory, and reflect how they have come to know the text.[8]

The majority of the books included in this exhibition are not manuscripts of the Bible, but books of other types, which were chosen to illustrate some of the principal sources of knowledge of the Bible in the twelfth century. The types of manuscripts included are representative; the selection of individual manuscripts was of course often determined by the contents of the collection. Liturgical books, exhibited in cases 2 and 3, are represented here by a manuscript containing fragments of a Missal and a Breviary, a number of lectionaries for the Mass and Divine Office, and fragments containing part of the Office of the Dead and the Hours of the Virgin. A selection of commentaries on the Bible follows in cases 4-7. Patristic commentaries, which were read liturgically and which formed the basis for most medieval commentaries through the twelfth century, are represented most fully, but the books included in this group in no way represent all the important commentaries of either the patristic or medieval periods. Cases 8 and 9 contain examples of

Glossed Books of the Bible. The Ordinary Gloss on the Bible, a re-ordering of the patristic and early medieval heritage, which adapted earlier commentaries to the new needs of the twelfth century, was the century's most important contribution to the history of biblical scholarship. Finally, the two manuscripts in case 10, Peter Comestor's *Historia scholastica*, and Peter of Poitiers' *Compendium historiae in genealogia christi*, must serve as examples of biblical commentaries by twelfth-century masters.

BIBLIOGRAPHY on Morimondo: A. C. Sangiuliani, "L'abbazia di Morimondo nella storia et nell'arte," *Rivista di storia benedettina* 3 (1908) 588-607 and 4 (1909) 41-55; Jean Leclercq, "Les peintures de la Bible de Morimondo," *Scriptorium* 10 (1956) 22-26 and plates 1-6; A. R. Natale, "Miniatura e codici cisterciensi del secolo XII," *Aevum* 32 (1958) 253-261.

NOTES:

[1] Edited by Jean Leclercq, O.S.B., "Manuscrits cisterciens," 173-181. Previously printed in J. Martini, Cat. 22 (1931), no. 12, pp. 12-13.

[2] Select bibliography of works pertaining to Morimondo listed below.

[3] Leclercq, "Manuscrits cisterciens," 176-177, nos. 1-5 and notes b and c; see also J. Leclercq, "Les peintures de la bible de Morimondo," *Scriptorium* 10 (1956) 22-26, discussing Côme, Seminario Maggiore MSS (IX-5) and (X-6), likely two volumes of the multi-volume Bible listed here.

[4] This catalogue was also edited by Leclercq from Vatican, MS Barberini 3229, f. 463; see Leclercq, "Manuscrits cisterciens," 181-182.

[5] Dom Leclercq's edition of the library catalogue in fMS Typ 223 includes indications of the present location of the books listed there; cf. Jean Leclercq, O.S.B., "Manuscrits cisterciens dans des bibliothèques d'Italie," *Analecta sacri ordinis cisterciens* 7 (1951) 71-75, including 10 manuscripts from Morimondo, now in Côme, Seminario Maggiore.

[6] The very angular script of fMS Typ 223 may be compared with that of Cambridge, Fitzwilliam Museum, McClean MSS 116-117, Origen, Commentary on the Old Testament (see M. R. James, *A Descriptive Catalogue of the McClean Collection of Manuscripts in the Fitzwillian Museum* [Cambridge 1912] 253-4, and plate LXXV). Somewhat less angular are the hands in former J. R. Abbey Collection, MS 7369, Sacramentary for Cistercian Use, datable between 1185 and 1191, with numerous later additions (see J. J. G. Alexander and A. C. de la Mare, *The Italian Manuscripts in the Libary of J. R. Abbey* [New York 1969] pp. 9-11, no. 3, and plate V), and Cambridge, Fitzwilliam Museum, McClean MS 113, Jerome, Commentary on Matthew, and McClean MS 8, Prophetae latinae (see James, pp. 246-7 and plate LXXI, and p. 13, plate 4).

[7] The script and decoration of Cambridge, Fitzwilliam Museum, McClean MS 29, Glossed Epistles, (see James, *Descriptive Catalogue*, 52-3 and plate XX), is even more characteristically "Italian" than that of MS Richardson 2 and fMS Typ 702.

[8] Leclercq, "Manuscrits cisterciens," 174; cf. also Jean Leclercq, "Saint Bernard et la tradition biblique d'après les Sermons sur les Cantiques," *Sacris erudiri* XI (1960) 225-248, especially 235.

diervo · ht · ɔ̃ · ū · c · Incip prefatio
eusebii ieronimi in ezram.

trum diffic
lius sit face
re quod pot
ctis an nega
re: necdum
statui. Nam
neq; uobis aliquid impariti
bus abnuere sententie est: &
magnitudo oneris impositi
tta ceruices premit. ut ante
sub fasce ruendum sit qm le
uandum. Accedunt ad hoc
inuidorum studia qui omne
quod scribimus reprehen
dendum putant: & interdu
contra se conscientia repug
nante publice lacerant que
occulte legunt. intantu ut
clamare compellar. & dicere.
Dne libera animam mea a

Plate 2. No. 2. fMS Typ 315, recto. 7/10 actual size.

14

2. Initial from a Bible

Northern France (Pontigny?) 1170s (?)   fMS Typ 315

Parchment, uneven cutting from a larger manuscript, trimmed on all sides; cut from the upper part of the page, with a few letters of one column, and the text of the other column remaining; now approximately 297-287 x 155-149, written space of one column (276 x 110) mm. 2 columns, 22 lines. Ruled visibly in brown crayon, with the top 2 and 15th and 16th lines full across, with only these horizontal rules extending across the space between the two columns. Reconstruction of physical make-up of the manuscript before it was cut: written space, (372 x 244) mm. 2 columns, 30 lines. Ruled in brown crayon with the top 2, middle 2, and bottom 2 horizontal rules full across.

Written above the top line in a formal, mature twelfth-century minuscule.

Six-line initial constructed from thin, intricate interlace, blue with touches of beige on an orange ground; initial extends into the upper margin, and terminates in a loose spiral with acanthus leaves, and a tail-less "dog"; infilled with similar interlace, entwined around the initial, in blue and beige, with large floral motif in center and pseudo-acanthus leaves in muted shades. Red rubrics. Purchased by Philip Hofer from Quaritch, London, July, 1956. Deposited by Hofer in the library, 1 January 1967; accession record: *68M-150 (120). Hofer bequest, 1984.

ONE OF THE OUTSTANDING achievements of the twelfth century was the production of monumental Bibles, usually copied in several volumes, and often lavishly decorated. Bibles of this type were copied in monasteries throughout Europe, functioning as glorious embodiments of the word of God, as well as more worldly symbols of the corporate identity of the monasteries that owned them. The initial shown here is the only example of this type of Bible in the library.[1]

Although only a fragment of one page remains, the original dimensions of the leaf can be reconstructed from an examination of the text and the ruling. This initial once belonged to a very impressive Bible copied in two columns of 30 lines, with a written-space measuring 372 x 244 mm., and outer dimensions probably very close to those of the thirteenth-century Bible also included in this case (fMS Typ 119; cat. no. 3). This painted initial is the beginning of Jerome's prologue to the book of Ezra. It is likely that the biblical books themselves were introduced by even more lavish initials, which illustrated scenes from the biblical books.

This initial has been ascribed to the Cistercian house of Pontigny in Burgundy.[2] Pontigny was famous for its library, and we will return to this very important monastery when we discuss MSS Richardson 14 and Typ 200 (cat. nos. 24 and 25). Fragments of a twelfth-century Bible from Pontigny do survive, including the nine leaves, now Paris, Bibliothèque Nationale, MS lat. 8823.[3] Three initials which have turned up in sales during the last thirty years may also be remnants of this great Bible.[4] Although at this time it is impossible to assert definitely that the cutting exhibited here is from the Pontigny Bible, an examination of the published material suggests that further study of the possibility would be worthwhile.[5]

No bibliography for this manuscript.

NOTES:

[1]Text as follows: [recto; stichometric indication from the end of 2 Chronicles] //dierum. habet versus $\bar{\text{ii}}$ c. [Jerome, Prologue to 1 Ezdras; Stegmüller 330] *Incipit prefatio eusebii ieronimi in ezram.* Utrum difficilius sit facere quod poscitis . . . Domine libera animam meam a// [verso] //statim ab omnibus conspuendum sit. Frustra autem ut ait . . . nisi emendatio librariorum dili//[gentia]

[2]Philip Hofer's notes on the manuscript, housed in the library, indicate that O. Pächt suggested the initial was from Pontigny, and could by dated c.1160-70.

[3]See Walter Cahn, *Romanesque Bible Illumination* (Ithaca, New York 1982) p. 277, cat. no. 91 and fig. 137, citing earlier bibliography.

[4]Listed by Cahn (cited above): two initials, formerly in the Hachette collection, now in a German private collection (Bournemouth, Alan G. Thomas, Cat. no. 4, 1958, p. 2, no. 3 and plate 2); and the initial sold at Sotheby's, London, 5 December 1978, lot 8, with plate.

[5]The initial published in A. G. Thomas' catalogue seems closest to fMS Typ 315.

3. Bible (fragments)

Northern France s. XIII[3/4]   fMS Typ 119

Parchment (good quality), ff. 6 (modern foliation, 1-6, bottom, outer corner, cited; foliation top, outer corner, recto, 5, 3, 4, 6, 2, 16, does not reflect the original order), 488 x 348 (335 x 228) mm. 2 columns, 30 lines. Ruled in lead with the top 3, middle 3 and bottom 3 lines full across; single full-length vertical bounding lines. Prickings, inner margin only.

1[5] (ff. 1 and 4, and 2 and 3, conjugate pairs, f. 5 is single); amount of text missing at the beginning and between ff. 4 and 5, suggests a reconstruction of the quire as follows: 1[12] (-1, 2, 3, and 4, before f. 1; and -9, 10 and 11, following f. 4); + 1 single leaf, now f. 6, from another quire. F. 5 is signed, middle bottom margin, "I," with horizontal catchword, bottom, inside margin.

Written below the top ruled line in a formal gothic bookhand.

One historiated initial, f. 4, at the beginning of Genesis, full-length of the page, with small vignettes depicting 7 days of creation and the Crucifixion; borders, top and bottom margins, with grotesques and drolleries. Two 5- to 6-line painted initials, f. 3 (prologue to Genesis) and f. 6v (Deuteronomy prologue). Chapters begin with blue 2-line initials with red pen decoration. Red and blue used for running titles and for roman numerals numbering the chapters; red rubrics. Purchased by Philip Hofer from E. Rosenthal, 1943. Hofer bequest, 1984.

THIRTEENTH-CENTURY MANUSCRIPTS of the Bible, in contrast with those copied earlier in the Middle Ages, were markedly smaller, and usually contain the complete text of the Scriptures. MS Lat 264, included in this case (cat. no. 6) is an example of a typical thirteenth-century pocket Bible. Nonetheless, very large, multi-volume Bibles were occasionally copied, as demonstrated by the leaves shown here. Coincidentally, these thirteenth-century leaves are probably very close in size to the original dimensions of the large twelfth-century Bible from which the initial, fMS Typ 315 (cat. no. 2) was cut. The two manuscripts are quite unrelated. The similarity of their formats, however, underlines the fact that both were created to serve similar functions, although almost a century separates them.

fMS Typ 119 now consists of only six leaves, containing portions of Jerome's introductory prologues to the Old Testament and Genesis, part of Genesis and part of Deuteronomy.[1] A few more leaves of this same Bible survive in other collections in this country.[2] Although the remainder of the manuscript has disappeared, its original appearance can to some extent be reconstructed by examining a group of related Bibles, also copied in the region of Northern France and Flanders, which are associated with the towns of Arras, Lille, Cambrai, and Tournai.[3] The evidence of these Bibles suggests that it was probably copied in four volumes, with volume one containing Genesis through Ruth, volume two, Kings through Job, volume three, Proverbs through Malachi, and volume four, Maccabees and the New Testament. Bibles such as these can best be seen as the continuation of twelfth-century traditions of book making into the thirteenth century. These thirteenth-century Bibles, like the large monastic Bibles of the previous century, were particularly suited for use by religious communities, and we can easily imagine a monk or nun reading aloud from such a book during meals.

BIBLIOGRAPHY: Faye and Bond, 260; *Harvard Cat.* (1955) p. 14, no. 26, and plate 15 (reproducing f. 4); Robert Branner, "A Cutting from a Thirteenth-century French Bible," *The Bulletin of the Cleveland Museum of Art* 58 (1971) 221, and n. 15, and 224-225; Anton Euw and Joachim Plotzek, *Die Handschriften der Sammlung Ludwig* (Cologne 1979) 1:99-103.

NOTES:

[1]Text as follows: ff. 1-4v [ff. 1-3 Jerome, general prologue (Stegmüller 284), here beginning imperfectly:] //[ser]uos dei et ancillas, id est super centum uiginti credentium nomina . . . [f. 3-4 Jerome, prologue to Genesis; Stegmüller 285] *Incipit prologus sancti hieronimi super penthateucum. Desiderii mei desideratas accepi epistolas* . . . [f. 4rv Genesis 1:1-29, ending imperfectly:] . . . *et uniuersa ligna que habent in semet ipsis sementem generis*//; f. 5rv [Genesis 6:4- 7:17, beginning and ending imperfectly:] //[fili]as hominum illeque genuerunt . . . et multiplicate sunt aquae et eleuauerunt arcam in//; f. 6rv [Deuteronomy 33:10 — end, beginning imperfectly:] //super altare tuum. Benedic domine fortitudini eius et opera manuum illius suscipe . . . [f. 6v Jerome, Prologue to Joshua; Stegmüller 311, here ending imperfectly:] *Incipit prologus sancti hieronimi presbiteri super librum ihesu naue id est iosue filii nun. Tandem finita pentatheuco moysi* . . . *ad ruth quoque et hester quos eisdem nominibus efferunt*//

[2]Robert Branner, "A Cutting from a Thirteenth-century French Bible," *The Bulletin of the Cleveland Museum of Art* 58 (1971) 221, notes 16-18, listing the following leaves: initials for Numbers and Joshua, given to the National Gallery of Art in Washington by Lessing J. Rosenwald (see Faye and Bond, 127, nos. 6 and 7); initial for Judges, Philadelphia Museum of Art, 46-65-1, given by Lessing J. Rosenwald, and Leviticus initial, described in the sales catalogues of H. P. Kraus, no. 7, pls. X and XI, and William H. Schab, Cat. 30, no. 2, with plate; this fragment is very likely to be identified with MS I.10, formerly in the Ludwig Collection, now in the J. Paul Getty Museum, Los Angeles, California, described in Anton Euw and Joachim Plotzek, *Die Handschriften der Sammlung Ludwig* (Cologne 1979) 1:99-103; Euw and Plotzek also mention another leaf with the beginning of Ruth in the possession of E. Rosenthal, Lugano, Switzerland.

[3]Cf. Robert Branner, "A Cutting," 220-221; Euw and Plotzek, *Die Handschriften Sammlung Ludwig* 85-98, discussing M33 I.8 and I.9, and related Bibles; Eleen Beer, "Liller Bibelcodices, Tournai und die Scriptorien der Stadt Arras," *Aachener Kunstblätter* 43 (1972) 190-226; Beer, "Das Scriptorium des Johannes Philomena und seine Illuminatoren," *Scriptorium* 23 (1969) 24-38; and Willene Clark, "A Re-united Bible and thirteenth century illumination in Northern France," *Speculum* 50 (1975) 33-47.

4.   Bible: Genesis — 4 Kings
England (?) s. XII^med-3/4   MS Typ 3

Parchment (fairly thin), ff. i (top quarter only remains) + 120, 265 x 171 (210-205 x 130-126) mm. 2 columns, 50 lines. Ruled in lead, usually with the top, the third from the top, the bottom, and the third from the bottom horizontal rules full across; through f. 197, only these horizontal rules extend across the space between the 2 columns; full-length vertical bounding lines, triple between the columns and double on the far inside and outside. Prickings top, bottom (cut away on some folios) and outer margins; quires 1 and 2 only (through f. 16v) also pricked in the inner margin.

1-15⁸. Horizontal catchwords, inside bottom edge, quires 4 and 13 (ff. 32v and 104v); partial remains of signature, bottom edge, left of center, verso of last leaf of quire 1 (f. 8v, "us" abbreviation only remains, roman numeral "I" probably cut away).

Written above the top line in a twelfth-century minuscule; script is small and compressed, but letter forms are conservative (upright 'd,' straight 's,' round 2-shaped 'r' usually used only after 'o,' e-cedilla used for 'ae,' ampersand usually used for 'et'); elongated and decorated ascenders used in the top line of script on each folio.

Books begin with 9- to 5-line blue, blue with decorative void space within the initial, or parted red and blue initials, with contrasting pen decoration (except initial f. 108, 4 Kings, in red); initial for Numbers, f. 37, omitted (1-line blank space remains). Chapters begin with 1-line initials placed within the written space at the beginning of a new line, often extending into the margin, in red, blue, green, parted red and green, or red and blue (ff. 57-end, only red or blue used for initials), many terminating in simple "arabesque" motifs, or with simple pen decoration in contrasting colors; 1-line initials in the same colors, placed within the line of text, are also used in some books. Red rubrics, often introduced by a red or blue paragraph mark; opening line of each book copied in red or blue capitals; running titles in red (often cut away); red or blue line-fillers. Owned by Philip Hofer; his gift to the library, 1942. Secundo folio: qui occidit cain.

THE RELATIVELY SMALL and compact format of this manuscript, which includes the beginning of the Old Testament, sets it apart from most twelfth-century Bibles. The absence of prologues and chapter lists, standard accompaniments to the biblical text at this time, can be most easily explained as a by-product of the attempt to minimize the size of the manuscript. Its text is divided into numerous short chapters, differing from those in use today. Except in the case of the Gospels (cf. cat. no. 5), references to the Bible at this time were only rarely identified by chapter numbers; indeed, so many different systems of chapter divisions were in use that such references would have been of little value. As is the case in many twelfth-century Bibles, therefore, all of the chapters in this manuscript are unnumbered, except for the final three chapters in Exodus, which are numbered as chapters 147, 148 and 149 on ff. 28v-29. It is difficult to think of an explanation of this anomaly. Perhaps the scribe's exemplar had numbered chapters, and he inattentively copied the numbers in this one spot. It is worth noting, however, that the layout of the manuscript emphasizes the chapter divisions. In most cases, the scribe began each chapter on a new line with a brightly colored initial, a practice not unknown in twelfth-century Bibles, but unusual enough to be worth noting. When chapters were accepted as standard units of reference in the thirteenth century, this layout was adopted in the majority of Bibles. Together with its compact size, the

pmo die pma mſt. erigeſ tabernaculū teſtimonii.
& poneſ in eo archā. dimitteſq; ante illā uelam.
Et illatam mſam. poneſ ſup eam que rite pcepta
ſt̃. Candelabrū ſtabit cū lucniſ ſuiſ. & altare au
reum in q̃ adoleie inceſum coia archa teſtimonii.
Tentorum in introitu tabnaculi poneſ. & ante illud
altare holocauſt. Labrū int̃ altare & tabnacu
lū. q̃d implebiſ aqua. Circūdabiſq; atrum tenou
riuſ. & ingreſſum eĩ. Et aſſumpto uctionis oleo ungeſ
tabnaculum cum uaſiſ ſuiſ ut ſcificent. Alta
re holocauſt & omĩa uaſa eĩ. Labrū cem baſi ſua.
Omĩa unctionis oleo conſecrabiſ ut ſint ſca ſcozum.
Applicabiſq; aaron & filioſ eĩ ad foreſ tabnaculi te
ſtimonii. & lotoſ aqua indueſ ſciſ ueſtib; ut mini
ſtrent m. & uncto coz in ſacdotium pficiat ſemp
cnum. fecitq; moyſeſ omĩa que pcepat dñſ. Cap̃ ltint.
Gĩo menſe pmo anni ſcdi in pma die mſiſ. colloca
tum .t̃. tabnaculum. Erexitq; illud moyſeſ. & poſu
it tabulaſ ac baſeſ & uecteſ. Statuitq; colūpnaſ.
& expandit cectum ſup tabnaculam. impoſito de
ſup opimento. ſic dñſ imparat. Poſuit & teſtimoni
um in archa. ſubditiſ mfra uectib;. & oraclu deſup.
Cumq; introtuliſſet archā in tabnaclm. appendit ant̃
eā uelu. ut ex pleret dñi iuſſionē. Poſuit & mſam
in tabnaculum teſtimonii ad plaga ſeptentriona
le ext̃ uelum. ordinatiſ coram ppoſitionis panib;.
ſicut pcepat domin̄ moyſi. Poſuit & candelabrū
in tabnaculum teſtimonii e regione mſe in par
te auſtrali. locaciſ p ordinē lucernis. iuxta pcep
tum dñi. Poſuit & altare aureū ſub tecto teſti
monii contra uelu. & adoleuit ſupillud inceſu
aromatū. ſic iuſſerat dñſ. Poſuit & tentorium in
introtu tabnaculi. & altare holocauſti in ueſtibulo te
ſtimonii. offerenſ in eo holocauſtū & ſacficia. ut dñſ
imparat. Labrūq; ſtatuit in tabnaculum teſti
monii & altare. impleſit illud aqua. Lauerūtq;
moyſes & aaron ac filii eĩ man̄ ſuaſ ſac pedeſ
cũ ingrederentur tectum fedïſ. & acceſſerent ad alta
re. ſic pcepat dñſ. Erexit & atrium p girum ta
bnaculi & altariſ. ducto in introitu eĩ tentorio. exlit.
Poſtquam cuncta pfecta ſunt. opuit nubeſ tab
naclm teſtimonii. & gła dñi impleuit illud. Nec po
tat moyſeſ ingdi tectum fediſ. nube opiente omĩa.
& maieſtate dñi choruſcante. q̃a cuncta nubeſ opu
erat. Siqñdo nubeſ tabnaclm deſerebat. pficiſce
bant̃ filii iſrł p turmaſ ſuaſ. Si pendebat deſup.
manebaut in eod̃ loco. Nubeſ q̃ppe dñi incubabat
p diem tabnaculo. & igniſ in nocte uidentib; po
puliſ iſrł p cunctaſ manſioneſ inaſ. Explit
belleſemoth. i d̃e exodus. h̃t uerſuſ. iii.

Incipit liber vaietra. quē noſ leuiticū dicim̃.
VOCAVIT AUTEM
dñſ ad Moyſen
& locutuſ .e̅. ei dñſ
de tabnaculo teſtimo
nii dicenſ. Loquere filiiſ
iſrł & diceſ ad eoſ. homo
qui optulerit ex uobiſ hoſtiam dño de pecoribz. ide
de bobz. & ouibz. offerenſ uictimaſ: ſi holocauſtum
fuerit eĩ oblatio ac de arīo. maſculum immacu
latū offeret ad oſtium tabnaculi teſtimonii. ad pla
candū ſ dñm. ponetq; manuſ ſup caput hoſtie. &
acceptabiliſ erit. atq; in expiatione eĩ pficienſ. Im
molabitq; uitulum coram dño. & offerent filii aaron
ſacerdotiſ ſangnem eĩ. fundenteſ p altariſ ccuitum
q̃d .e̅. ante oſtium tabnaculi. Detractaq; pelle hoſtie.
artuſ in fruſta concident. & ſubicient in altari igne
ſtrue lignoꝛ. ante compoſita. & mbra que ceſa ſt̃
deſup ordinanteſ. caput uidelicet & cuncta que
adherent iecoꝛi. inteſtiniſ & pedibz lotiſ aqua.
adolebitq; ea ſacerdoſ ſup altare in holocauſtū &
ſuaue odoꝛem dño. Quod ſi de pecoribz oblatio .e̅. de
ouibz ſiue de capꝛiſ. holocauſtū annicłm & abſq; ma
cula offeret. immolabitq; ad latuſ altariſ. q̃d reſpicit
ad aq̃lonem coram dño. Sangnē u̅ iłi fundent ſup
altare filii aaron p cuitum. diuidentq; mbra. caput
& omĩa que adherent iecoꝛi. & imponent ſup ligna
quib; ſubiciendaſ .e̅. igniſ. Inteſtina u̅ & pedeſ la
uabunt aqua. & oblata omĩa adolebit ſacerdoſ
ſup altare in holocauſtū. & odoꝛem ſuauiſſimū
dño. Si aut̃ de auib; holocauſti oblatio fuerit.
dño. de turturib; & pulliſ columbe: offeret eam
ſacerdoſ ad altare. Et reuocato ad collum capite ac rup
to uulniſ loco. decurrit facet ſangnē ſup crepidinē
altaris. Veſiculam u̅ gutturiſ & plumaſ pieet ppe
altare ad oientalem plagā. in loco in quo cinereſ ef
fundi ſolent. Confringetq; aſcellaſ eĩ. & ñ ſecabit
nec ferro diuidet eam. & adolebit ſup altare lig
niſ igne ſuppoſito. holocauſtum .e̅. & oblatio ſua
uiſſimi odoꝛis dño. Anima cum optulit oblatio
nem ſacficii dño. ſimila erit eĩ oblatio. fundetq;
ſup eam oleū & ponet thuſ. ac deferet ad filioſ
aaron ſacerdotis. quoꝛ un̄ tollet pugillū plena
ſimile & oleï ac totum thus. & ponet memou
ale ſup altare in odoꝛem ſuauiſſimū dño. Quod
aut̃ reliquum fuit de ſacficio. erit aaron & fi
liozum eĩ. ſcm ſcoꝛum de oblationibz dño. Cum
aut̃ optuliſ ſacficiam coctum in clibano de ſi
mila. paneſ ſcilicet abſq; fermēto conſpſoſ oleo.
& lagana azima oleo lita. ſi oblatio tua fūt

layout of this book would have made it a useful volume for personal reading and for reference, thus anticipating the developments of the next century.

The history of this manuscript from the early fourteenth century is well documented. It is included in the catalogue of the Benedictine cathedral priory of Christ Church, Canterbury, compiled by the Prior, Henry of Eastry. The manuscript is described there as the "Eptaticus Iohannis de Bokking," with a list of its contents, Genesis through 4 Kings.[1] There is little doubt that this is our manuscript. On the front flyleaf there is an inscription in a thirteenth-century hand beginning, "Eptaticus Johannis"; the following word is erased, but the last letters, "king" can be discerned under ultra-violet light. The description of the book as a "Heptateuch," the first seven books of the Bible, is inaccurate, a fact noted on the same page in the comment: "Summa in universo xii libri et ideo dicitur eptaticus."[2] The book's location in the library is recorded on the same page, "D[istinctio] iii. G[radus] iiii," referring most likely to the book press and shelf, respectively. The book remained at Christ Church, and the names of a number of fifteenth-century monks are recorded on the flyleaves.[3] The manuscript's presence at Christ Church in the early fourteenth century, however, is not proof that it was made there. In fact, the description of the book as "John of Bokking's Heptateuch," may indicate that John gave the book to the Abbey. Given the manuscript's interesting format and layout, further research as to its likely provenance would be especially interesting.

BIBLIOGRAPHY: De Ricci, 1692 (= New York, Collection of Philip Hofer, MS 1); Faye and Bond, 250.

NOTES:

[1] Printed in M. R. James, *The Ancient Libraries of Canterbury and Dover* (Cambridge 1903) 13-149, with MS Typ 3 listed on p. 27, nos. 99 and 100; see also N. R. Ker, ed., *Medieval Libraries of Great Britain; A List of Surviving Books* (London, 2nd. ed. 1964) 34.

[2] James assumed that since no. 99 in Eastry's catalogue was described as a Heptateuch, the four books of Kings listed immediately following was another manuscript, which he numbered 100, and identified as Trinity College, Cambridge MS B.4.30 (see James, 507). Neil Ker noted James' error after examining MS Typ 3 in January 1969 (correspondence in library files).

[3] The following names were identified by Neil Ker, in correspondence, January 1969, after a visit to the library: front flyleaf, f. i, and f. 120v: "Si hic perdatur Arnoldo Permisted restituatur"; Arnoldus Permisted was monk of Christ Church, d. 1464; back flyleaf, f. i: "Si quis istum inuenerit librum Johanne covintre restituat monacho"; Johannes Covintre was professed in 1465 (see also, Ker, *Medieval Libraries of Great Britain,* 239; De Ricci, 1692, incorrectly interpreted this to mean that the manuscript once belonged to the Hospital of St. John at Coventry); inside back cover, "Robert Ykham," professed in 1464.

5. Gospel Book
Italy s. XII[1]   MS Riant 20

Parchment (very well prepared in the manner of Southern Europe; thin and even), ff. v + 179 + v, 95 x 62 (71-69 x 43-39) mm., except ff. 1-2, (71 x 48-46) mm. 25 long lines. Ruled in hard point, with the top 2 and bottom 1 horizontal rules full across; single full-length vertical bounding lines; some folios with an extra vertical bounding line in the outer margin next to the prickings, used to align the indications of the Eusebian sections. Slash-type prickings in the top and outer margins.

1[12] (-12, following f. 11, excised, with loss of text) 2-8[10] 9[10] (through f. 91v, with prologue to Luke ending imperfectly; possibly once with an additional single leaf, now lost) 10-15[12] 16-17[8].

Written above the top line in a minute, even caroline minuscule; e-cedilla used consistently for 'ae,' round 's,' 'r'and 'd' are avoided, and the ampersand is used to abbreviate 'et' both as a single word and internally.

Each Gospel begins with a full page painted frontispiece, ff. 12, 62, 92 and 143, with large, 17- to 22-line geometric-style initials in pink-red, blue and green, outlined in brushed gold and terminating in interlace; the text is continued in smaller decorative capitals, surrounded by narrow full-page borders with interlace in different colored blocks, acanthus leaves, roundels, etc. Sections within the text begin with 3- to 1-line red initials, painted over with brushed gold. 1-line initials within the text; red rubrics. Canon tables enclosed in simple brushed gold and red rectangular frames. Belonged to Comte Paul Riant (1836-1888); his manuscripts given to Harvard in 1900 by J. Randolph Coolidge and Archibald Cary Coolidge. Secundo folio: ad eius exemplum.

THE MOST REMARKABLE FEATURE of this book is its extraordinarily small size. It is, as far as I know, a unique phenomenon. Much more typical of Italy in the eleventh and twelfth centuries are the well-known "Giant" Bibles — monumental copies of the entire Bible, which usually measure about 550 x 380 mm.[1] Gospel Books were commonly copied in a more modest format, but they were still considerably larger than our manuscript. The script and decoration of this manuscript are very conservative; a date in the first half of the twelfth century, rather than in the eleventh century, is suggested by the very thin and evenly finished parchment. Sophisticated parchment of this quality made the production of such a tiny volume possible.[2] Where this remarkable manuscript was produced, and why, are intriguing but still unanswered questions. None of the usual categories of use and ownership seem to fit this book. It would obviously have been unsuitable for any sort of public reading of the Gospels. It is carefully written and decorated, and shows no signs of having been used for private study. Moreover, since it is inevitably more precious and remarkable than truly impressive, one wonders if a Bishop or important lay ruler would have considered it worth owning.

The four Gospels in this manuscript are accompanied by a number of non-biblical texts. The manuscript begins with a copy of Jerome's letter to Pope Damasus, written in 383 or 384, summarizing the difficulties Jerome encountered while revising the text of the Gospels.[3] A set of Canon Tables follows, enclosed in simple gold and red rectangular frames. The Canon Tables, compiled in the fourth century by Eusebius of Caesarea, compare the text of the four Gospels by indicating which

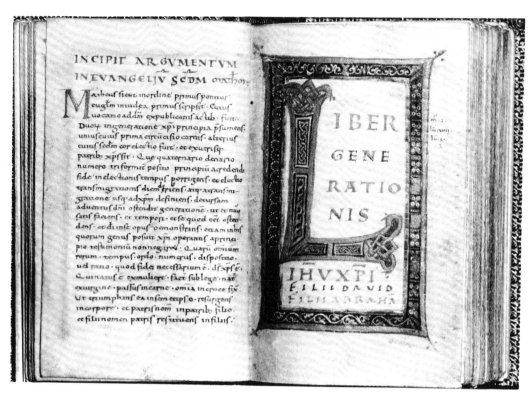

Plate 4. No. 5. MS Riant 20, ff. 11v–12. Actual size.

passages are found in all four Gospels, which are found in only three, and continuing in like manner. They conclude with lists of passages unique to each gospel. In the Canon Tables themselves each passage is indicated by a number, corresponding to short sections of the text of the Gospel which are numbered in the margins. It should be noted that the sections used by Eusebius to divide the Gospels do not correspond to the chapters used in Bibles today. Jerome's letter and the Canon Tables were included in virtually every copy of the Gospels up to the thirteenth century. The Gospels are introduced by short prologues, or arguments, which discuss the Evangelists and their reasons for composing the Gospels.[4] These prologues are very old, probably dating from the fourth century, and written in very difficult Latin. Scholars today have shown that they were probably written in heretical circles. Given the extreme obscurity of their language, it is not surprising that no one in the Middle Ages questioned their orthodoxy, and they circulated in manuscripts of the Bible into the sixteenth century.

BIBLIOGRAPHY: De Ricci, 1002; L. de Germon and L. Polain, *Catalogue de la bibliothèque de feu M. le Comte Riant, deuxième partie* (Paris 1899) vol. 1, p. xlix, no. 20; W. F. Wyatt, "Riant 20: A Description" (unpublished manuscript, Cambridge, Massachusetts 1912) now Houghton bMS Lat 315(29).

NOTES:

[1] See Henri Quentin, *Mémoire sur l'établissement du texte de la Vulgate; première partie: Octateuque.* Collectanea biblica latina, 6 (Rome and Paris 1922) 361-380; E. B. Garrison, *Studies in the History of Medieval Italian Painting, I-IV* (Florence 1953-1962).

[2] We thank Professor R. H. Rouse, September, 1986, for his suggestions in dating this manuscript.

[3] Stegmüller 590; English translation in W. H. Free-

mantle, *St. Jerome. Letters and Selected Works.* A Select Library of Nicene and Post Nicene Fathers 2nd Series 6, P. Schaff and H. Wace, eds. (New York 1893) 487-488.

[4] Stegmüller 590, 607, 620, and 624. The most recent discussion of the monarchian prologues is found in J. Regul, *Die antimonarcionitischen Evangelienprologue. Vetus latina; die Reste der altlateinischen Bibel. Aus der Geschichte der lateinischen Bibel* 6 (Freiburg i. Br. 1969).

6. Bible

France (Paris) s. XIII^{med} MS Lat 264

Parchment (extremely thin), ff. i + 632 + i, 162 x 112 (114-113 x 75-73) mm. 2 columns, 45 lines. Ruled in lead, with the top horizontal line usually full across, and with a set of horizontal rules full across in the upper margin for the running headlines; full-length single vertical bounding lines. Some prickings, top margin.

1-4^{24} 5^{22} 6-8^{24} 9^{26} 10-11^{24} 12^{22} 13-17^{24} 18^{20} 19-24^{24} 25^{20} (-19, after f. 588, cancelled, with no loss of text) 26^{20} 27^{20} (+ 1, f. 630, after 20) 28^{2}. Some leaf signatures, blue letters, bottom right margin, recto, visible in quires 23 and 25 (beginning on ff. 523 and 571).

Written below the top line in a minute pointed gothic book hand by several scribes. Later notes and corrections throughout.

Two historiated initials of fair quality, extending beyond the length of the written space, with simple border extensions of rinceaux and dragons in blue and dark red on grounds of these colors, with touches of green, salmon and brown: f. 1 (General prologue) Jerome writing; and f. 4v (Genesis) seven days of creation and the Crucifixion. Attributed to the Mathurin atelier, active in Paris, c.1230 — c.1250 (see Robert Branner, *Manuscript Painting in Paris During the Reign of Saint Louis* [Berkeley 1977] p. 214 and fig. xiii, reproducing f. 4v). Simple rinceaux initials, 3- to 6-line with extensions, for the remaining books and prologues, the beginning of Daniel 13, and major divisions within the Psalms. Chapters and remaining Psalms with 2-line initials, alternating red and blue, set into the text column, with pen flourishes of the other color. Running headlines in red and blue majuscules throughout, except in the Psalter and *Interpretation of Hebrew Names.* Chapters numbered within the text columns with red and blue roman numerals. Red rubrics; majuscules in text usually touched with red. Some guide letters indicating the chapter initials in the inner margins; notes in lead for running headlines. Belonged to Charles Sumner (1811-1874). Acquired by Harvard, Sumner bequest, April 28, 1874; formerly MS Sumner 55. Secundo folio: veram [corr.: vera] sapientia perdet.

THIS SMALL VOLUME is representative of a remarkable historical change.[1] The Bible as we know it today, consisting of the complete Scriptures from Genesis to the Apocalypse, conveniently divided into chapters, and usually copied in a small format so that it can easily be used for reference and carried about, was an invention of the thirteenth century. This manuscript is, of course, in Latin, and the style of the writing and the decoration may seem foreign. Nonetheless, problems of language and style aside, this Bible is remarkably similar to Bibles in use today. Acts here follows the Pauline Epistles instead of the Gospels, but otherwise the biblical books are arranged in the same order as the modern Bible. The chapters are also basically the same as those used today, although the chapters are not divided into verses, which were a sixteenth-century innovation. Running titles at the top of every page aid the reader in finding his or her place. The small, rather chunky shape of this book is one still used for many printed Bibles, especially editions of the Latin Vulgate.[2]

All of these features were new in the thirteenth century. They should be seen in the context of the most significant innovation of all, the number of Bibles copied in the thirteenth century. The many hundreds of little Bibles similar to this one that survive stand in stark contrast to the small number of Bibles copied in the twelfth century. The importance of the Bible in the twelfth century can hardly be overemphasized, but as this exhibition demonstrates, the Bible then was largely a public book, known through recitation, through the liturgy, and through the study of commentaries on the text. The Bible in the thirteenth century, for the first time in the Middle Ages, was a privately owned book, available to the educated clergy and perhaps to very wealthy lay people, for study, reading, and reference.

BIBLIOGRAPHY: De Ricci, 1015 (= MS Sumner 55); Faye and Bond, 244; J. Winsor, ed., "The Collection of Books and Autographs Bequeathed to Harvard College Library by the Honorable Charles Sumner," *Library of Harvard University. Bibliographical Contributions* 1 (1879) 16, col. b, no. 7. FURTHER READING: for an account of the textual history of the Bible in the thirteenth century, citing earlier studies, see L. Light, "Versions et révisions du texte biblique," in *Le Moyen Age et la Bible*, P. Riché and G. Lobrichon, eds. Bible de tous les temps 4 (Paris 1984) 75-93.

NOTES:

[1]The order of the books and the choice of prologues conforms to the usual pattern found in Bibles from northern France dating after c.1230 (cf. Ker, *Medieval Manuscripts in British Libraries* [Oxford 1969] 1:96-7). A test of the characteristic readings listed by H. Quentin in *Mémoire sur l'établissement du texte de la Vulgate, première partie: Octateuque.* Collectanea biblica latina 6 (Rome 1922) 385, indicates that textually it is related to the family of the "University" or Paris Bible.

[2]Christopher de Hamel, *A History of Illuminated Manuscripts* (Boston 1986) 113-117.

7. Missal and Breviary (fragments)

Italy s. XII[1]   MS Typ 413

Parchment (many repairs, holes, etc.), ff. i + 89 (rebound after 1955 and the leaves rearranged; previous order as follows [using present foliation]: ff. 28-33; 9-27; 34-89; 1-8) + i, 223 x 135 mm. Layout varies: ff. 1-6 (Ordinary of the Mass), written space (164 x 92-85) mm. 27 long lines; ff. 7-8v, 10-24, 26-89 (remaining leaves contain later additions), written space (164-157 x 90-87) mm. 37-36 long lines. Ruled in hard point, with the top 1 or 3 and the bottom 1 or 3 horizontal rules full across on most leaves; double full-length vertical bounding lines. Prickings in three outer margins (some cut away).

1[6] (1 and 6 are single) 2[4] (all single) 3[6] 4[8] (3, f. 20, and 6, f. 23, are single; +1, f. 17, inserted before 1) 5-10[8] 11[8] (3, f. 76, and 6, f. 79, are single), break in text suggests that quires are missing between 11 and 12, 12[8].

Written on the top line in a twelfth-century minuscule; letter forms tend to be square in shape; 'ae' written together or as e-cedilla.

Two orange initials, ff. 1 (Common Preface) and 1v (Canon), occupying roughly half the page, ending in interlace, and infilled with a white vine, with the spaces between the vine in orange, yellow and brown. 4- to 2-line red initials, often with decorative terminals; 1-line red initials within the text. Red rubrics. Purchased from Erik von Scherling (see *Rotulus* VII, no. 2476) in 1955 (Hofer fund). Accession record: *55M-102. Secundo folio: memento domine.

THE LITURGICAL OBSERVANCES of the Church were one of the principal sources of knowledge of the Bible throughout the Middle Ages. Two biblical readings, one from the Gospels, and one from another book of the Bible, usually the Epistles, are part of each Mass. The core of the Divine Office, the public prayer of the Church said by members of the monastic orders and by priests, is the recitation of the psalter, which is said completely each week. Readings from the other books of the Bible, as well as from biblical commentaries, also form part of the Office.

The manuscript shown here contains portions of both a Missal and a Breviary, the main service books for the Mass and the Office. Missals, the earliest of which date from the eighth or ninth century, contain all the texts necessary to celebrate the Mass, including the Ordinary of the Mass, the Prefaces and the Canon, and the variable prayers, chants, and biblical readings. Portions of the services were also copied in independent volumes. The Sacramentary, for example, contains only those portions of the Mass said by the celebrant at High or Solemn Mass. The traditional description of this manuscript as a Sacramentary is incorrect.[1] Examples of Evangeliaria, which contain only the Gospel readings for the Mass, are also included in this case (see cat. nos. 8 and 9).

Breviaries contain Psalms, lessons, and prayers for the Office. Like the Missal, the Breviary is a compendium, which gathers together material from different volumes, such as Lectionaries, Psalters, and Antiphonaries. Examples of the different types of manuscripts which include only the lessons for the Office are also exhibited here (see cat. nos. 10-13). The earliest Breviaries were copied in the eleventh century.

25

In both the books for the Mass and those for the Office, the variable portions of the text are arranged in three sections. The Temporale, or Proper of the Time, contains Sundays and the feasts celebrating the life of Christ, many of which are moveable and occur on different dates each year, such as Easter. The Sanctorale, or Proper of the Saints includes the feasts of saints, as well as the feasts in honor of the Virgin Mary. The Common of the Saints supplements the Sanctorale, and contains material for general categories of saints, such as confessors, martyrs and virgins.

The manuscript shown here is now in fragmentary condition. It opens with the Ordinary of the Mass, that is, the prayers of consecration said during each Mass, here arranged with the Common Preface, followed by the Canon, and the variable prefaces.[2] It also includes a large portion of the prayers which change depending on the time of year and the feast, here arranged with the Temporale and Sanctorale combined. This section is not complete.[3] Most intriguing is the inclusion on ff. 10-24 of a portion of the Common of the Saints from a Breviary.[4] These leaves are very similar in script, decoration and layout to the rest of the manuscript. Manuscripts combining services for the Mass and the Office are very rare, but it is possible that our manuscript was once such a combined Missal and Breviary.[5] Alternatively, it may be the remnants of two independent, but very similar, volumes, a Missal and a Breviary, which are now bound together. Given the present fragmentary condition of the manuscript, it is impossible to determine which of these explanations is more likely.

BIBLIOGRAPHY: Faye and Bond, 276; Harvard College Library, *The Houghton Library, 1942-1967. A Selection of Books and Manuscripts in Harvard Collections* (Cambridge, Mass. 1967), p. 178, plate of f. 1v. FURTHER READING: Josef A. Jungman, *The Mass of the Roman Rite*, English translation of 2nd German edition, 2 vols. (New York 1951-2); Pierre Batiffol, *History of the Roman Breviary* (London 1912); Pierre Salmon, *The Breviary through the Centuries* (Collegeville, Minn. 1962).

NOTES:

[1]Described as a Sacramentary in Faye and Bond, 276. Described as a Breviary and Sacramentary in *Rotulus* VII (1955) no. 2476, with the text on ff. 34-89v (now ff. 26-81v) and ff. 1-8 (now ff. 82-89v), actually parts of a Missal, incorrectly described as fragments of a Breviary.

[2]Ff. 1-6.

[3]Ff. 26-81v, from the first Sunday in Lent to Saturday in the fourth week of Lent, ending imperfectly; ff. 82-99v, from the 12th through the 22nd Sunday after Pentecost, beginning imperfectly.

[4]Monastic use; major feasts include three nocturns, each containing four lessons.

[5]Cf. Andrew Hughes, *Medieval Manuscripts for Mass and Office: a Guide to their Organization and Terminology* (Toronto 1982) 303-305, appendix 7, discussing combined Breviaries and Missals.

8. Evangeliary: Gospel Lectionary for the Mass

Italy (Morimondo?) s. XII^{med-3/4} (before 1174/5)   fMS Typ 210

Parchment, ff. iii + 173 (incorrectly foliated by an earlier hand in roman numerals in faded ink, upper, outside corner, 1-79, 90*-181; correct foliation in modern hand, cited) + iii, 292 x 200 (207-203 x 125-120) mm. 18 long lines. Ff. 1-64v, ruled in very hard lead, usually leaving only faint traces of black, with the top 1 or 2 and bottom 1 or 2 horizontal rules full across; single full-length vertical bounding lines; ff. 65-end, ruled visibly in lead, with the top 2, middle 2, and bottom 2 horizontal rules full across; double full-length vertical bounding lines. Prickings in top, bottom and outer margins.

1-21⁸ 22⁸ (-6, 7, 8, possibly with loss of text).¹ Signed in roman numerals, often flourished, middle, very bottom margin, verso of last leaf in quire (many cut away). Horizontal catchwords, inside, bottom margin (many cut away).

Written on the top line, by at least two scribes, with the second beginning on f. 65, in a mature twelfth-century minuscule; round 'd,' 's' and 'r' used frequently; 'ae' written 'e.'

Major initials, used for important feasts, and in the Exultet text, begin with 11- to 6-line bold blue, red or green initials, infilled with patterns in green, orange and blue, interspersed with white decorative space, or decorated with stripes or dots; some with simple pen decoration. Secondary initials, 6- to 4-line blue, green, or red-orange, with decorative void spaces, dots or simple pen flourishes in contrasting colors; fanciful zoomorphic initials in the same style for some feasts, for example, f. 9v (fish), f. 29v (winged-serpent), f. 108 (winged-horse), etc. Red rubrics with opening letters often in green or blue. Ff. 80v-85 (Exultet text) with staff for musical notation with alternate red and green lines, notation in black, and with red and brown used for alternate phrases in the text. Majuscules within the text daubed with red. Accented for oral reading in red. Some notes for the rubricator remain, written vertically along the outside edge. Belonged to Philip Hofer, who purchased the manuscript from L. C. Harper, Inc. in April, 1953. Hofer bequest, 1984. Secundo folio: suum. Et ecce angelus.

IN MANY CHURCHES AND MONASTERIES during the Middle Ages the daily Gospel lesson for the Mass was sung from a copy of the Gospels. Lists, known as *capitularia*, recording the passage to be used each day, are often found at the beginning or end of Gospel Books, and the readings were marked in some way within the text itself. This system, however, had certain disadvantages, since the Gospels are not read continuously during the year, but rather are chosen for their suitability to the particular feast. The accounts of Christ's Passion, to pick an obvious example, are chanted during the last week in Lent, culminating on Good Friday. From a very early time, therefore, the text of the Gospel lessons, or pericopes, were excerpted from the Gospels and arranged in the order of the liturgical year. Books containing these lessons are known as Evangeliaria. In parallel fashion, collections known as Epistolaries were assembled which contained the first lesson of the Mass from the Epistles and other biblical books.

The type of script and style of decoration in this Evangeliary are similar to those in the Office Lectionary, fMS Typ 223 (cat. no. 10), also in this case, which was copied in the Cistercian monastery at Morimondo in Northern Italy.² A striking feature of both of these manuscripts is the numerous marginal notes, added by many different people over a long period of time, beginning very shortly after they

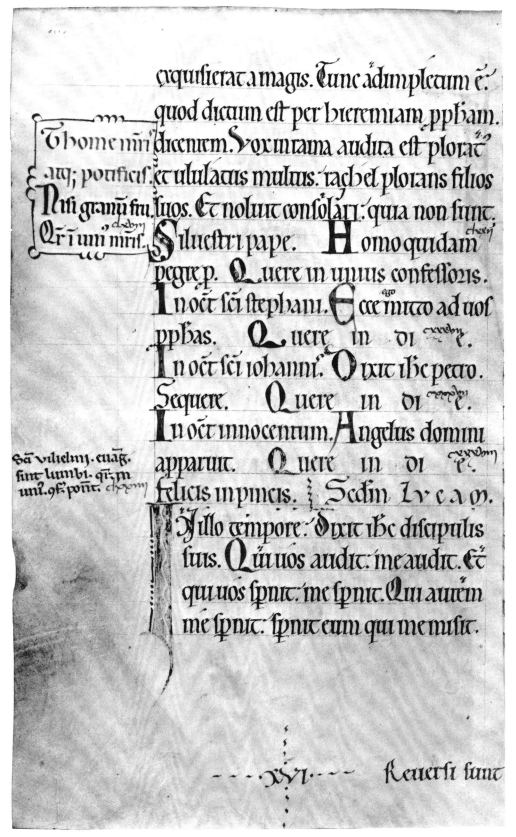

exquisierat a magis. Tunc adimpletum e̅: quod dictum est per hieremiam. ppham. dicentem. Vox in rama audita est plorac̅ aq̅; pontificis. et ululatus multus. rachel plorans filios suos. Et noluit consolari. quia non sunt. Siluestri pape. Homo quidam pegre p. Quere in unius confessoris. In oct̅ sci stephani. Ecce mitto ad uos ppbas. Quere in di xxxviij. In oct̅ sci iohannis. Dixit ihc petro. Sequere. Quere in di xxxviij. In oct̅ innocentum. Angelus domini apparuit. Quere in di xxxviij. felicis in pincis. ¶ Secdm Lvca m.

Thome mr̅ aq̅; pontificis.
N̅ sti granm̅ fru.
Qr̅ i uni̅ mrtis.

Sa̅ vilielmi. euag̅. sunt lumbi. qr̅ in uni̅.9f. pont.

In illo tempore: Dixit ihc discipulis suis. Qui uos audit: me audit. Et qui uos spnit: me spnit. Qui autem me spnit: spnit eum qui me misit.

- - - - - xvi - - - - Reuersi sunt

Plate 5. No. 8. fMS Typ 210, f. 128v. 7/10 actual size.

28

were copied, and continuing through the fifteenth century. The care to keep these books up to date as new feasts were added to the liturgy, as well as their worn condition, especially evident in the frequent repairs in the bottom margins, testify to the fact that they were actively used in the Abbey's Church throughout the Middle Ages; one can guess that they were retired to the library only after the monastery acquired printed copies of these texts. The similarity of the content of these additions provides proof that both of these manuscripts date from approximately the same time,[3] and, moreover, provides supporting evidence that this Evangeliary was indeed copied at Morimondo, as suggested by Wormwald in 1956.[4]

An unusual feature of this manuscript is the inclusion of the Blessing of the Paschal Candle before the Gospel lesson for Holy Saturday, a text which one would not expect to find in a Gospel Lectionary.[5] The very ancient and beautiful text, which, like the Gospel pericopes, was sung by the deacon, begins "Exultet iam angelica turba coelorum," "Let now the heavenly hosts of angels rejoice." It is copied here with the musical notation, and decorated with especially elaborate initials. This is the same text that is found in the beautiful illustrated Exultet rolls copied in Southern Italy from the tenth through the thirteenth centuries.

BIBLIOGRAPHY: De Ricci, 1161, no. 4 (= New Jersey, Collection of Acton Griscom, MS B.29); Faye and Bond, 270; *Harvard Cat.* (1955) p. 11, no. 10 and plate 7 (reproducing f. 81v). FURTHER READING: on the Exultet rolls, see M. Avery, *The Exultet Rolls of South Italy* (Princeton 1936); and G. Cavallo, *I Rotoli di Exultet dell' Italia meridionale* (Bari 1973).

NOTES:

[1]Text ends in the Common of the Saints, with the third reading for the dead, John 5:21-24; further texts may have followed.

[2]The smaller initials in fMS Typ 223 (for example f. 56) are similar to those in fMS Typ 210; cf. also former Collection of J. R. Abbey, MS 7369, Sacramentary for Cistercian Use, s. XII (described in J. J. G. Alexander and A. C. de la Mare, *The Italian Manuscripts in the Library of Major J. R. Abbey* [New York 1969] pp. 9-11, no. 3, and plate V). In his edition of the twelfth-century book list of Morimondo found in fMS Typ 223 (see cat. no. 1), Dom Leclercq suggested that no. 54, "item duo euangeliaria," might be identified with Tuxedo Park, New York, Collection of Gronville Kane, MS 1, a copy of the Gospel of Mark (described in De Ricci, 1889), and Vatican City, Biblioteca Apostolica Vaticana, MS Vat. lat. 10680, Luke (see M. Vattaso and E. Carusi, *Codices Vaticani Latini*, vol. 5 [Rome 1920] 647); the possibility could be raised whether one of the books referred to is fMS Typ 210, since it is followed in the list by other liturgical books. Nos. 30 and 31 in the inventory, "Lectionarii duo unum de dominicis et alterum de festis," have been interpreted as referring to Princeton University Library, MS 6 (described in De Ricci, 1177), and to fMS Typ 223.

[3]Trinity Sunday, included in the original hand in the Temporale, was officially observed in the Cistercian Order beginning in 1175; Bernard, canonized in 1174, and with a proper office since 1175, was here omitted from the original text. It is likely, therefore, that the manuscript was copied not long before 1174. It may be noted that Thomas Becket, F. 29 December, canonized in 1173, and observed in the Cistercian order in 1185, is also added.

[4]Pencil note in manuscript in Philip Hofer's hand. Unlike the other Morimondo books in the library this MS is bound in nineteenth-century black morocco, rather than in Morimondo's characteristic heavy wooden boards covered with smooth, brown leather (see cat. no. 1).

[5]Ff. 80-85.

9. Evangeliary: Gospel Lectionary for the Mass

Italy (Northern?) s. XII^med-3/4   fMS Typ 138

Parchment (fine and even), ff. ii + 88 (foliated 1-87, + 1 unnumbered leaf) + i, 307 x 206 (201-198 x 120-116) mm.[1] 20 long lines. Ruled in hard point with the top 2 and bottom 2 horizontal rules full across; single full-length vertical bounding lines. Some prickings, bottom margin.

1² (conjugate pair) 2-11⁸ 12⁴ 13² (conjugate pair; 2, f. 88, unnumbered). Horizontal catchwords, lower, inside margin.

Written on the top line in a very round "reformed" Italian twelfth century minuscule; 'ae' represented by e-cedilla; round 'd' and round 's' used occasionally; uncial forms used for the rubrics and capitals within the text.

Twelve 12- to 6-line pale yellow geometric-style initials, infilled with bright colored patterns on stepped grounds of brown or bright blue, at the beginning of major feasts; initial, f. 33v, terminates in a red bird, drawn in outline. Remaining Gospel texts begin with 5- to 3-line red initials, plain or simply decorated. Red rubrics. Purchased, January, 1948, from Lathrop C. Harper, N.Y., by Philip Hofer. Deposited by Hofer in the library, 1 January 1967; accession record: *68M-150(28). Hofer bequest, 1984. Secundo folio: f. 2 (added, s. XIII¹) Adesto domine; f. 4 (originally f. 2) [in]fantem pannis.

THE TEXT OF THIS EVANGELIARY is organized in the traditional manner, with the texts for the Temporale, followed by the Sanctorale and the Common of the Saints. The Temporale here begins with the readings for the Vigil Mass on Christmas Eve and the three Christmas Masses, which in the twelfth century were taken from the well-loved accounts of the birth of Christ, as they still are today. Matthew, chapter 1 was read at the Vigil Mass on Christmas Eve, and Luke, chapter 2, was begun at the midnight Mass and continued at the Mass at dawn; the majestic first chapter of John was read during the third Mass on Christmas Day. The custom of beginning the liturgical year on Christmas Eve was an ancient one; by the twelfth century, many liturgical books begin with the first Sunday in Advent, a custom still followed today. The accounts of the Passion read on Palm Sunday and Good Friday are marked in this manuscript with small red letters (p, c, and s), indicating the speakers. Today different readers are chosen for each of these parts; in the Middle Ages the text was often chanted by one person, using different pitches for each part.[2]

Two leaves were added to the manuscript early in the thirteenth century, with prayers to various saints, including Homobonus. A merchant from Cremona, known for his honesty and piety, Homobonus died in 1197, and was canonized shortly thereafter in 1199. Homobonus became the patron saint of Cremona, and the inclusion of prayers to him suggests that the manuscript was in Cremona early in its history. The round, very clear and elegant script of this manuscript, and the style of its decoration, known to art historians as the "geometric style," are both associated especially with Central Italy and Tuscany; this style was not, however, unknown in Northern Italy, and it is possible that this manuscript was copied in Cremona.[3]

BIBLIOGRAPHY: De Ricci, 1161, no. 5 (= New Jersey, Collection of Acton Griscom, MS It.25); Faye and Bond, 263; *Harvard Cat.* (1955), p. 11, no. 12, plate 6 (reproducing f. 33v, incorrectly identified as f. 133v).

NOTES:

[1]Ff. 1v-2v were added in an Italian hand, s. XIII[1]; physical description as follows: written space: (c. 200 x 113-110) mm. 20 long lines. Ruled in hard point with the top 2 and bottom 2 horizontal lines full across; single full-length vertical bounding lines. Copied in an early Gothic bookhand, in 2 sizes depending on liturgical function. 2- to 1-line red initials with crude red pen flourishes set outside the written space; red rubrics.

[2]This manuscript uses "p" to designate Christ, "c" for the narrator, and "s" for the crowds and disciples; the usual designation for Christ is a cross or "t"; cf. John Plummer, *Liturgical Manuscripts for the Mass and the Divine Office* (New York 1964) 17, no. 12.

[3]Cf. for example, Francois Avril and Yolanta Załuska, *Manuscrits enluminés d'origine italienne, 1: VIe — XIIe siècle* Bibliothèque Nationale, Département de manuscrits, Centre de récherche sur les manuscrits enluminés (Paris 1980) p. 69, no. 117 and plate XLVII (Paris, Bibliothèque nationale, MS lat. 797), p. 70, no. 120 and plates XLVII and XLVIII (Paris BN MS lat. 654), both decorated in the geometric style, and likely from Northern Italy; nos. 119 and 124 described in this catalogue could also be cited. The type of script used in this manuscript is discussed below, see cat. no. 12 and note 3.

10.   Office Lectionary
Italy (Morimondo) s. XII[med-3/4] (before 1174/5).   fMS Typ 223

Parchment, ff. i + 233 (modern foliation, upper, outer corner in pencil, 1-227, + 6 leaves added between ff. 103-104, foliated separately, I-VI, cited; medieval foliation in red roman numerals remains on some folios, copied as part of the running title on the recto) + i, 370 x 240 (272-270 x 159-154) mm.[1] 2 columns, 28 lines (some folios in the first quire ruled for 29 lines, but with 28 lines of text). Ruled, usually quite heavily, in lead with the top 3, middle 3 and bottom 3 horizontal rules extending full across in the outer margin; all horizontal rules usually extend full across on the inside; full-length vertical bounding lines, single in the inner and outer margins, and triple between the columns. Prickings, bottom margin only.

1-9[8] 10[8] (-8, following f. 79v, cancelled with no loss of text) 11-13[8] (through f. 103v) 14[6] (added leaves, foliated I-VI; II/III and IV/V, conjugate pairs, inserted into I/VI) 15-29[8] 30[4] (singletons). Quires signed, bottom margin between the columns, verso of last leaf, "primus," "secundus," etc., flourished on all sides, and often bracketed by paragraph marks; horizontal catchwords, bottom, inside margin, some with paragraph marks (catchwords and signatures cut away in some quires).

Written on the top line in a formal, twelfth-century minuscule; tops of letters such as 'm' and 'n' are smooth, but finishing strokes, shape of 'o,' etc., give the script a markedly sharp and broken appearance; 'ae' often written e-cedilla; both round and straight 's' are used; 'd' usually upright; decorative letter forms used for majuscules.

Feasts begin with large 10- to 5-line (except f. 1, 14-lines) red or blue initials, with many types of pen decoration including interlace, acanthus scrolls, and light, feathery strokes for shading in black, red, blue, green, or pale yellow. Lessons begin with 3- to 2-line red, blue, or green initials with simple pen decoration. Red rubrics. Majuscules within the text brushed with pale yellow. Running titles, in red, with foliation in roman numerals on the recto, remain on some folios (possibly added). Purchased from J. Martini (Cat. 22, 1931, no. 12) by Philip Hofer. Hofer bequest, 1984. Secundo folio: [re]demptoris. Ostendit.

THE DIVINE OFFICE consists of seven services, said at specified times during the day and night, beginning with Matins at approximately 2 a.m., and continuing with Lauds, Prime, Terce, Sext, None, Vespers, and concluding with Compline at sunset. Matins is the longest service. Following a series of introductory prayers, it is divided into a number of parts, known as nocturns, each of which contains Psalms and lessons. The number of nocturns varies depending on liturgical custom and the type of feast. On Sundays and major feasts in Benedictine Monasteries, and in other orders following their practices, Matins includes three nocturns, each with four lessons. A Gospel reading follows the twelfth lesson. On weekdays during the winter the service consists of two nocturns, the first with three lessons, and the second with a short lesson, known as a chapter, which Benedict specified was to be said from memory; in the summer, the first nocturn for weekdays has only one reading. Manuscripts with twelve lessons for major feasts, and either three or one lesson for weekdays, therefore, are monastic in provenance. According to secular use, Matins consists of one to three nocturns, depending on the rank of the feast, each with three lessons. On major feasts, therefore, nine lessons were read at Matins, whereas on weekdays only three were read.

The content of the lessons read at Matins varied a great deal during the Middle Ages. In theory, the lessons of the first nocturn were taken from the Bible, the lessons of the second nocturn from patristic commentaries or sermons, and those for the third nocturn from a homily on the Gospels. In practice, however, many exceptions to this pattern are found. Lives of the saints were often substituted for the other types of readings, and readings from the Fathers or other authors often replaced the Scriptural readings of the first nocturn.

The manuscript shown here, an Office Lectionary, contains the lessons for Matins for the feasts of the Sanctorale and the Common of the Saints. The text begins with the lessons for the feast of Stephen (26 December) and continues through the feast of Thomas the Apostle (21 December); the Common of the Saints follows. It was copied at the Cistercian Abbey of St. Mary at Morimondo in Italy.[2] We have already discussed the library catalogue from Morimondo, which was copied on the last leaf of this Lectionary at the end of the twelfth century (see cat. no. 1). The compiler of the catalogue noted that the monastery owned two lectionaries, one for Sundays and one for feasts; the latter is likely a reference to this manuscript.[3] The lessons follow the pattern one would expect to find in a monastic manuscript, with twelve lessons given for major feasts, followed by the reading from the Gospels. Like the Gospel lectionary, f MS Typ 210 (cat. no. 8), which we have suggested is also from Morimondo, this manuscript includes numerous marginal additions, which kept the text up to date as the liturgy changed.[4]

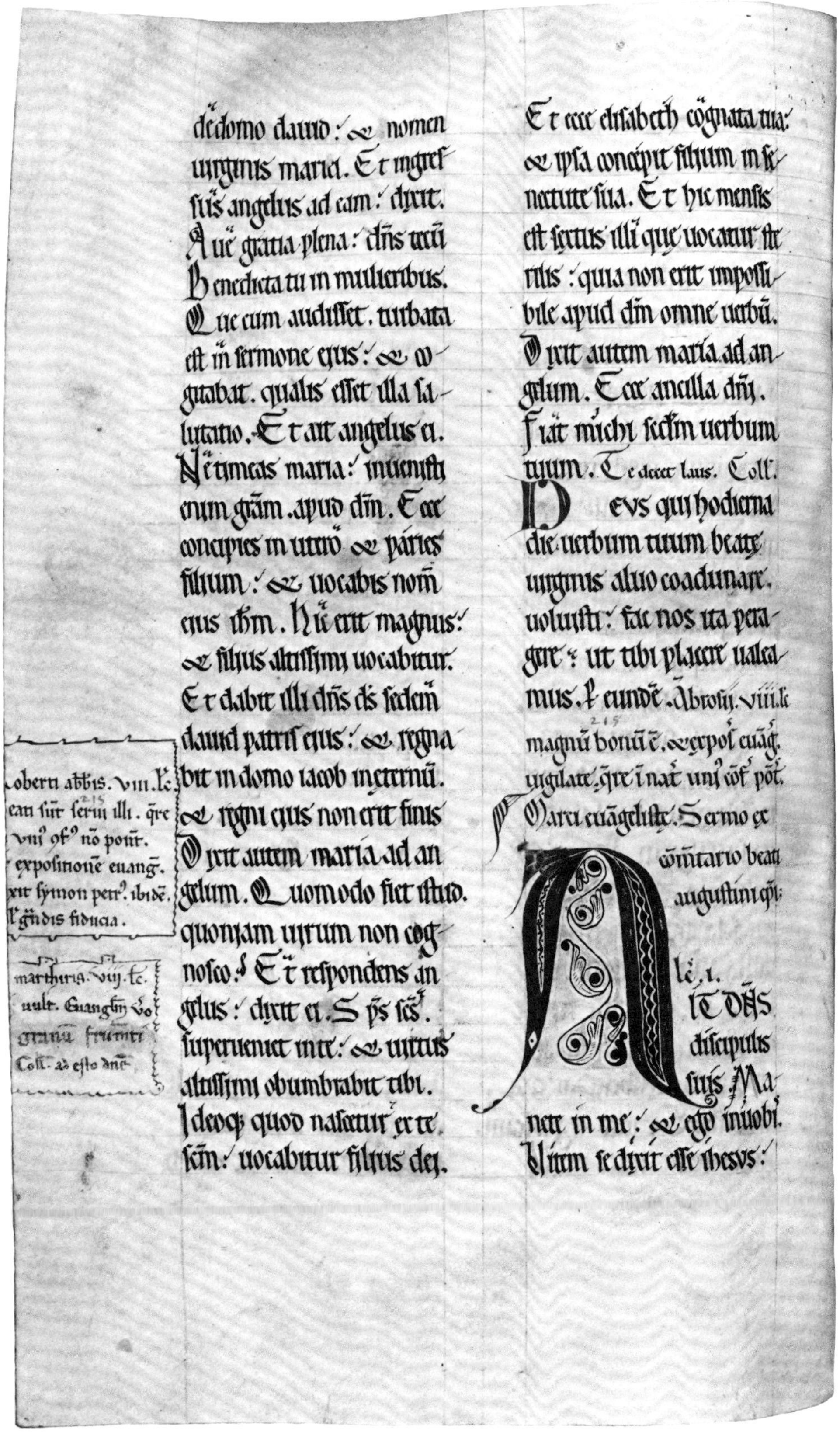

de domo dauid: & nomen
uirginis marie. Et ingres-
sus angelus ad eam: dixit.
Aue gratia plena: dns tecu
Benedicta tu in mulieribus.
Que cum audisset. turbata
est in sermone eius: & co-
gitabat. qualis esset illa sa-
lutatio. Et ait angelus ei.
Ne timeas maria: inuenisti
enim gram. apud dm. Ecce
concipies in utero & paries
filium: & uocabis nom
eius ihm. Hic erit magnus:
& filius altissimi uocabitur.
Et dabit illi dns ds sedem
dauid patris eius: & regna-
bit in domo iacob ineternu.
& regni eius non erit finis.
Dixit autem maria ad an-
gelum. Quomodo fiet istud.
quoniam uirum non cog-
nosco? Et respondens an-
gelus: dixit ei. Sps scs.
superueniet inte: & uirtus
altissimi obumbrabit tibi.
Ideoq; quod nascetur ex te
scm: uocabitur filius dei.

obert abbis. viii. le
eati sut seru illi. que
uni of? no pout.
expositioe euang.
xit symon petr? ibide.
l' gndis fiducia.

marturis. vij. le.
ult. Euagliu bo
gnatu frumti
Coll. ad esto dne.

Et ecce elisabeth cognata tua:
& ipsa concepit filium in se-
nectute sua. Et hic mensis
est sextus illi que uocatur ste-
rilis: quia non erit impossi-
bile apud dm omne uerbu.
Dixit autem maria ad an-
gelum. Ecce ancilla dni.
fiat michi secm uerbum
tuum. Te decet laus. Coll.
Deus qui hodierna
die uerbum tuum beate
uirginis aluo coadunare
uoluisti: fac nos ita pera-
gere: ut tibi placere uelea-
mus. P eunde. Ambrosij. viii. le
magnu bonu e. &expos euag.
uigilate. &c. i nat uni cof pot.
Marci euageliste. Sermo ex
comitario beati
augustini epi
Ale. 1.
IT DNS
discipulis
suis Ma-
nete in me: & ego inuobi.
Ut iam se dixit esse ihesus:

Plate 6. No. 10. fMS Typ 223, f. 49v. 3/5 actual size.

33

Other types of manuscripts were also used for the readings at Matins, such as collections of patristic sermons (see cat. no. 12), and collections of homilies (see cat. no. 13); manuscripts of this type were also arranged according to the liturgical year. Indications of the lessons for Matins are also frequently found in the margins of copies of biblical commentaries which include no other signs that they were used liturgically. fMS Typ 703, a large copy of Augustine's Commentary on the Psalms included in the exhibition (cat. no. 15), is an example of this type of manuscript.

BIBLIOGRAPHY: De Ricci, 1693 (= New York, Collection of Philip Hofer, MS 5); Faye and Bond, 272; *Harvard Cat.* (1955) p. 11, no. 13 and plate 6 (reproducing f. 125).

NOTES:

[1]Physical description of quire 14 (ff. I-VI, between ff. 103-104), added, s. XII[2]: written space (280-285 x 160) mm. 2 columns, 29 lines. Ruled very lightly in lead, with the top 3 and bottom 2 or 3 horizontal lines full across; full-length vertical bounding lines, single on the inside and outside and triple between the columns. Written on the top line in upright, very formal minuscule; generally rounder in appearance than the script in the remainder of the manuscript. 2- to 3-line red and green parted initials with simple "shadow" pen decoration in green.

[2]Initials in this manuscript may be compared to those in Oxford, Bodleian Library, MS Canon. Pat. Lat. 214, Ambrose, Commentary on the Psalms (see Otto Pächt and J. J. G. Alexander, *Illuminated Manuscripts in the Bodleian Library, Oxford. 2. Italian School* [Oxford 1970] p. 5, no. 50

and plate V); and in Cambridge, Fitzwilliam Museum, McClean MS 8, Prophetae latinae (see M. R. James, *A Descriptive Catalogue of the McClean Collection of Manuscripts in the Fitzwilliam Museum* [Cambridge 1912] 13 and plate IV).

[3]Leclercq, "Manuscrits cisterciens," 178, no. 31.

[4]Additions indicate that it was copied before 1174/5, but likely fairly close to that date: lessons for Bernard, canonized in 1174, and with a proper office in 1175, are added on 6 leaves inserted between ff. 103-4, in a hand only slightly later than the remainder of the manuscript. Thomas of Canterbury, F. 29 December, canonized in 1173, and observed in the Cistercian order in 1185, is also added.

11. Office Lectionary ("The Oberwesel Lectionary")
Germany (diocese of Trier?) s. XII[4/4] — XIII[1]   MS Typ 444

Parchment (stiff; hair side dark and rough), ff. ii + 118 + ii, 300 x 207 (226 x 153-146) mm. 20 long lines. Ruled in lead, with the top 2 and bottom 2 or 3 horizontal rules full across; double full-length vertical bounding lines.

1-13[8] 14[4] (beginning on f. 105) 15[8] 16[2].

Written on the top ruled line in a large, even minuscule; 'ae' is often written e-cedilla; round 'd' is not used; round 'r' used only after 'o' and round 's' only at end of words; no letter unions.

Thirteen 5- to 4-line red initials (with 'I' extending up to 7-lines) used at the beginning of each major feast, with "arabesque" decoration in blue, yellow, brown and green; Trinity Sunday, f. 26, begins with a more elaborate 6-line initial. Remaining divisions indicated by 2-line undecorated red initials. Red rubrics. Purchased by the Library in 1958 from Martin Breslauer (Hofer Fund). Accession record: *57M-246. Secundo folio: uexillum domini.

SCVLETVR IN Assumptione s̄. d̄arie. Fant. cc̄or.

uos e osculo oris sui.' quia me l-.u.
luora sunt ubera tua uino.fra
glantia unguentis optimis.
Oleum effusum nomen tuū.'
ideo adolescentulę dilexerunt te. Tra
he me post te.' curremus in odore un
guentoꝝ tuoꝝ. Introduxit me rex ī
cellaria sua. Exultabimus ꝺ letabim̄
inte. oꝭmores uberū tuoꝝ sup̄ uinū.'
recti diligunt te. Nigra sum s; formo
sa filię iħrlm.' sicut tabernacula cedar.
sicut pellis salemonis. Nolite me consi
derare auod fusca sim.' quia decolora
uit me sol. Filii matris meę pugna
uerunt contra me. posuerunt me cus
todem inuineis.' uineā meā ñ custodiui.
Indica michi que̅ diligit ✝ ·ii.
anima mea. ubi pascas. ubi cubes in
meridie.' ne uagari in cipiam ꝑ greges

Like the Morimondo Lectionary (fMS Typ 223; cat. no. 10), this manuscript contains lessons for use at the office of Matins. The organization and contents of these manuscripts, however, differ significantly. The Oberwesel lectionary may have been compiled to supplement a full lectionary such as fMS Typ 223, by providing alternate sets of lessons for feasts already observed, or by supplying readings for new feasts. The text begins with lessons for the Invention of the Cross (May 3), a fixed feast usually found in the Sanctorale. It is followed, however, by three feasts, the Ascension, Pentecost, and Trinity Sunday, which one would expect to find in the Temporale, and by a series of lessons for the days of the week. The manuscript then returns to the Sanctorale with an uncommon feast, the Separation of the Apostles (15 July),[1] and continues with ten additional feasts, seemingly chosen at random from the Sanctorale, concluding with the feast of St. Nicholas (6 December). The lessons are taken from different sources; readings for some feasts are from Saints' Lives, for others, from the Bible or from patristic sermons and commentaries. In three cases, the text is continued after the final lesson. In 1920, Eric Millar identified the notes on f. 118v, which were added to the manuscript in two informal hands, presumably not long after it was copied, as originating at the Convent of All Saints at Oberwesel in the diocese of Trier.[2] The contents of the manuscript, however, suggest that it is possible that the manuscript was not copied at this house, but rather acquired by the nuns shortly after it was made. fMS Typ 233, as we have seen, includes twelve lessons for major feasts, with four lessons read at each of the three nocturns at Matins. The six lessons for major feasts included in the Oberwesel Lectionary were likely meant to be read during the first two nocturns; the lessons for the third nocturn must have been drawn from another source. This structure does not correspond to the liturgical practice followed in the Benedictine Order.[3]

The date of the Oberwesel lectionary is also an open question. Although it has traditionally been assigned a date in the twelfth century, it may have been copied in the thirteenth, perhaps as late as c.1240. The script is markedly "sharp" and broken in appearance, suggesting the influence of gothic bookhands,[4] but letter unions are avoided (except 'pp' which is occasionally joined), and letter forms are conservative. The majuscule letters used in the text, decorated by functionless pen strokes and distortions of the shapes of the letters, are especially striking, and strongly suggest that the manuscript was not copied during the twelfth century. Such combinations of earlier letter-forms and "gothic" ductus are characteristic of the scripts which continued in use in some parts of Germany well into the thirteenth century.

BIBLIOGRAPHY: Faye and Bond, 278-79.

NOTES:

[1] See ff. 42v-45v,"*In divisione apostolorum*"; we thank C. Dutschke for information about this feast.

[2] Typescript, dated April, 1920, now housed with the manuscript.

[3] The possibility exists that the liturgical practices at Oberwesel varied from the usual Benedictine use because it was a house for nuns. The convent was incorporated into the Cistercian order in 1259 (see *Gallia Christiana* 13:654).

[4] Note especially the manner in which detached strokes are used to form round letters, and the finishing strokes on minims and descenders. Trier, Dombibliothek, MS 133, a manuscript of Rufinus' translation of Eusebius, copied in 1191 in Trier, is similarly sharp and "broken" in appearance, although its decoration and the majuscule letters used in the text differ from those in Typ 444 (see Franz Steffens, *Lateinische Paläographie,* second edition [Berlin and Leipzig 1929] plate 86 of f. 2v; the manuscript is known to me only through this plate).

12. Sermologus, fragments
Central Italy s. XII[med]   fMS Typ 291

Parchment, ff. 3 (3 single leaves, trimmed on all sides, glued onto paper stubs), f. 1: 426 x 285-283 (393 x 242-235) mm. 2 columns, 50 lines; f. 2: 426 x 283-280 (393 x 244-237) mm. 2 columns, 50 lines; f. 3, unevenly cut, 387-385 x 284-280 (374-370 x 243-237) mm. 2 columns, 47 lines. Ruled in hard point. Horizontal rules are drawn across the center column, and often extend randomly beyond the vertical bounding lines; single full-length vertical bounding lines.

Written above the top ruled line in a round "reformed" twelfth-century minuscule; 'pp' written separately, round 's' and 'd' used occasionally, 'ae' usually written e-cedilla; majuscule letters based on uncial models.

One 6-line red initial, f. 2, with decorative void spaces and terminals. Purchased by Philip Hofer from Eric von Scherling, Leyden, in May, 1954. Deposited by Hofer in the library, 1 January 1967; accession record: *68M-150 (96). Hofer bequest, 1984.

THESE THREE LEAVES were once part of a larger volume containing a collection of patristic sermons arranged according to the liturgical year. The only remaining rubric notes that the sermon by Pope Leo on the Passion is to be used on "feria iv," or Wednesday, likely during Holy Week.[1] The sermons are copied without any indication of their division into lessons. They could have been read at meals in a monastic community, used as sources for sermons to be preached at Mass, or used for the readings of the Office at Matins. As we have seen, the lessons for either the first two nocturns or for the second nocturn, were often drawn from patristic sermons (see cat. no. 10).

The leaves shown here are representative of the handsome collections of homilies and sermons produced in great numbers in Central Italy and Tuscany in the twelfth century.[2] These manuscripts were very large, and copied in an extremely elegant script. The distinctively round letter-forms in the script used for the text in our manuscript, as well as the influence of uncial script on the majuscules and the display script, also observable here, are characteristic of these impressive Italian homiliaries.[3]

paulo ante commemoraui . quia prop
terea non du̅ erat sp̅s illo utiq̅ nouo .
modo post resurrectione̅ credentib₂
datus . quia ih̅s nondu̅ erat glorificat .
Id e̅ nondu̅ fuerat mortalitas in mor
talitate uestita et in ęterni̅ uirtute̅
temporalis infirmitas commutata .
potest deista clarificatione dictum
uideri . nunc clarificatus e̅ filius ho
minis . Ut quod ait nunc non ad immi
nente̅ passione̅ . set adiuicina̅ resurrec
tionem ptinere creditur . tanquam
fuerit factu̅ quod erat tam proxime
futurum FR . IIII . S̅C̅I S̅ LEONIS PP
ERMONE DE IN
glosi d̅ni n̅ri ih̅u xp̅i pas
sione promissum ita ex
pectationi u̅re intellego
ē̅ reddendu̅ . ut officiu̅
disserendi et festo paschu̅
seruiat et auribₕ impii erroris occur
rat . Qui eni̅ di filiu̅ u̅era n̅re carnis
negant suscepisse natura̅ . in imici sunt
fidei xp̅iane . et euanglicam predica
tionem nimis impudenter impugnant .
ut scdm ipsos crux xp̅i aut simulatio
fuerit fantasmatis . aut supplicium
deitatis quod acordibₕ pioru̅ longe e̅
repellendum . quia catholica integri
tas nec maculam pfidie nec ruga̅ potest
habere mendacii . que unu̅ xp̅m sic d̅m
sic homine̅ confitetur . ut nec falsum
homine̅ nec d̅m dicat fuisse passibile̅ .
Quia uis ergo abillo initio quo inuto
uirginis uerbu̅ caro factu̅ e̅ nichil um
quam interdiuina̅ humana̅q̅ substan
tium diuisionis extiterit . et p omia
incrementa corporea unius persone
fuerint totius te̅poris actiones . Ea
ipsa tamen que inseparabiliter facta
sunt nulla pmixtione confundimus .
sed quod cuius naturę sit exoperum
qualitate sentimus . Nec diuina enim
humanis preiudicant . nec humana̅
diuinis . cu̅ ita in ipsum utra̅q̅ concur
rant ut in eis nec proprietas assumat
nec psona geminetur . Transcursis igit
hisque habeat passione d̅ni precessere .
quid documentoru̅ habeat sacra̅tu̅
paschale tractemus . N̅a exardescente

ad effectus suis sceleris seuitia iudoru̅ .
Cu̅ ds c̅c̅ in xp̅o mundu̅ reconcilians
sibi nulla̅ uis te̅plo corporis eius nisi
pmitteret potuisset inferri . Siquide̅
terribilis illa militu̅ cohors et aprin
cipibₕ ac phariseis missa cu̅ gladiis et
fustibₕ multitudo ita una d̅m uoce
pculsa sit ut cu̅ turbe dixissent ih̅m
sequererent nazarenu̅ . respondisse̅tq̅
ego sum . nemo coru̅ subsisteret sed
om̅s simul amisso me̅nbroru̅ officio
retrorsum acti disi̅q̅ corruerunt . In
quo utiq̅ diuine erat potestatis indi
cium que impioru̅ conatus . non armis
contrarius ne̅q̅ ullus creaturę potenti
auxilio sed sola uerbi uirtute proster
neret . Quia uero saluando humano
generi alterius operis ratio congruebat
nec posset sanguis xp̅i pretiu̅ credentu̅
fieri si redemptor se non sinret co̅phendi
admisit adse impias manus . et cohibi
ta e̅ potentia deitatis ut pueniretur
ad gl̅am passionis . Cuius utiq̅ inanes
fuisse species . et nulli profutura imago
tollerantie nisi uera diuinitas ueris
se humane carnis sensibₕ induisset . Ut
unus dei atq̅ hominis filius aliunde
intemerabilis aliunde passibilis . mor
tale n̅rm psu̅a mortalitate renouaret .
Et ideo mestitudine . et ideo formidine
non caruit . ut adiciendas huiusmodi
pturbationes non solu̅ sacramento nos
susceptiones . sed et̅i exe̅plo formidinis
roboraret . N̅a iniusta uideretur eius
ad patientia̅ cogitatio . cui nulla . ē̅t
in n̅ra infirmitate co̅munio . Ueras aute̅
d̅ni passiones esayas ppha ipsius uoce
pronuntians dicens . Dorsu̅ meu̅ dedi
in flagella . et maxillas meas in palmas .
Uultu̅ aute̅ meu̅ non auerti a confusi
one sputoru̅ . Quod itaq̅ uerbi caro pa
tiebatur . non uerbi erat passa sed car
nis . Cuius iniurie atq̅ supplicia et iam
ad impassibile̅ redundabat ut merito
ei dicantur inlata que ipsius sunt
corpus admissa . dicente apto . Si eni
cognouissent . nu̅qua̅ d̅hm maiestatis .
crucifixissent . Obcecati eni iudei ma
licia in quod, prupissent facinus nesci
ebant . Unde misericors ih̅s qui etia̅

No bibliography on this item. FURTHER READING: Réginald Grégoire, *Homéliaires liturgiques médiévaux; analyse de manuscrits*. Biblioteca degli "Studi Medievale" 12 (Spoleto 1980).

NOTES:

[1]Sermon 65, text begins, f. 2, and here ends imperfectly, f. 2v; printed *PL* 54:361-364, and CC 138A, pp. 395-399.

[2]Compare for example, Knut Berg, *Studies in Tuscan Twelfth-Century Illumination* (Oslo 1968), p. 231, cat. no. 13, Florence, Bibl. Laurenziana, MS Plut. 14.1, Homiliary, Tuscany, s. XII$^{3/4}$, 545 x 360 mm.; p. 236, cat. no. 20, Florence, Bibl. Laurenziana, MS Plut. 16.41, Homiliary, Tuscany, s. XII$^{2/4}$, 480 x 305 mm.; p. 239, cat. no. 25, Florence, Bibl. Laurenziana, MS Plut. 17.39, Homiliary, Tuscany, s. XII^2, 540 x 360 mm.; and many other exam-ples of very large-format collections of homilies (see his cat. nos. 26, 27, 29, 41, 46, 48, etc.). Manuscripts such as these are comparable in size to Italian "Giant" Bibles (mentioned above, cat. no. 5).

[3]Cf. E. B. Garrison, *Studies in the History of Mediaeval Italian Painting* (Florence 1953) I:37-41, figs. 27-32; Garrison describes the script as "reformed script." fMS Typ 138 (cat. no. 9), fMS Lat 168 (cat. no. 27), and MS Typ 260 (cat. no. 31) are also copied in this distinctive type of script; fMS Typ 441 (cat. no. 13) was copied by a less accomplished scribe who used similar letter forms.

13. Homiliary, fragments
Central Italy s. XII^{med} fMS Typ 441

Parchment (darkened), ff. i + 16 + i, 320 x 239-234, unevenly trimmed, (247-245 x 170-162) mm. 2 columns, 30 lines. Ruled in hard point; horizontal rules generally extend full across into the gutter in the inner margin; in the outer margin the top 3 and sometimes the bottom 2 or 3 are drawn full across to the outer edge; single full-length vertical bounding lines. Prickings in three outer margins.

Two discontinuous quires of 8 from a larger manuscript; horizontal catchwords written near the bottom edge, to the right of the center.

Written above the top line in a round twelfth-century minuscule; round 'd' used frequently; 's' and 'r' are usually straight; 'ae' written e-cedilla. Majuscules are modelled on uncial letter forms.

Homilies begin with 2-line red initials (initials on ff. 8v and 10v are brown); scriptural passages preceding the homilies begin with 2-line brown or red initials. Rubrics in red uncials. Guide notes for rubricator, bottom edge, ff. 10 and 13. Beginning of lessons within the text marked by a cross in the margin in brown ink. Purchased, August 27, 1957 from H. P. Kraus (Hofer fund). Accession record: *57M-33F.

THIS MANUSCRIPT INCLUDES two discontinuous quires from a homiliary, that is, a collection of patristic homilies on the Gospels arranged according to the liturgical year for use at the third nocturn at Matins. Like fMS Typ 291 (cat. no. 12), it was probably copied in Central Italy around the middle of the twelfth century. The type of script used in both of these manuscripts is similar, although in this manuscript, a smaller, and generally less elegant volume, the script is less rounded and not as precise. The text of each homily is preceded by a brief summary of the Gospel text, and is divided into three readings indicated by crosses in the margin, which are either contemporary with the manuscript or early additions.

Only a fragment of the original manuscript survives. The first quire contains portions of the text for the Temporale, from the second through the fifth Sunday after Epiphany, concluding with the feast of the Purification (2 February). The second quire begins with the first Sunday "in quadragesima," or Lent, and continues through the fourth Sunday, here called "Dominica de lazaro," from the Gospel reading of the day, which recounts Christ's raising of Lazarus from the dead.[1]

BIBLIOGRAPHY: Faye and Bond, 278.

NOTES:
[1]Text in both quires begins and ends imperfectly.

14. Office of the Dead and Hours of the Virgin, fragments, in a fifteenth-century Office Book
Germany s. XII$^{4/4}$ MS Lat 282

Parchment, ff. 32, 207-205 x 144-140 mm., unevenly trimmed. Manuscript was assembled in the fifteenth century, in five physically distinct sections from a number of MSS: I. ff. 1-3v, fragment from another manuscript: 1^4 (-4, excised, with loss of text); II. ff. 4-20v: 2^8 (-1, before f. 4, with loss of text) 3^{10} (through f. 20); III. ff. 21-22v, litany and prayers: 4^2; IV. ff. 23-28v, twelfth-century leaves: 5^2 (singletons, glued to parchment stubs) 6^4; V. ff. 29-32: 7-8^2 (through f. 32v).

Ff. 23-28v, six twelfth-century leaves, with text on ff. 23, 25v-26, and f. 27mid-28v, scraped and rewritten in a fifteenth-century hand. Ff. 23-27 (excluding 15th-century additions): trimmed, with the top of the initial, f. 24v, cut away; written space (155-153 x 96-94) mm. 19 long lines. Ruled in brown crayon with the top 1 or 2 and bottom 1 or 2 horizontal rules full across; single full-length vertical bounding lines. Written above the top ruled line in a late twelfth-century minuscule in two sizes depending on liturgical function. 4- to 2-line brushed gold initials, outlined in red, with simple green pen flourishes, decorated with pale yellow. 1-line plain red initials; red rubrics.

Ff. 27mid-28v, and fifteenth-century additions in above section: written space (183-175 x 120-115) mm. 2 columns, 40-38 lines. Ruled in ink; single full-length vertical bounding lines. Written in a gothic text hand. 2-line red initials; red rubrics.

Bequeathed to the library in 1950 by Rosamond Bowditch Loring. Secundo folio: Dies absoluti.

THIS MANUSCRIPT IS A remarkable example of how complicated the history of a volume can be. The portion we are interested in consists of six leaves from a twelfth-century Psalter, Book of Hours, or Breviary, containing the Office of the Dead and parts of the Hours of the Virgin. These devotions were added to the Divine Office at a fairly early date, and reflect the structure of the main canonical

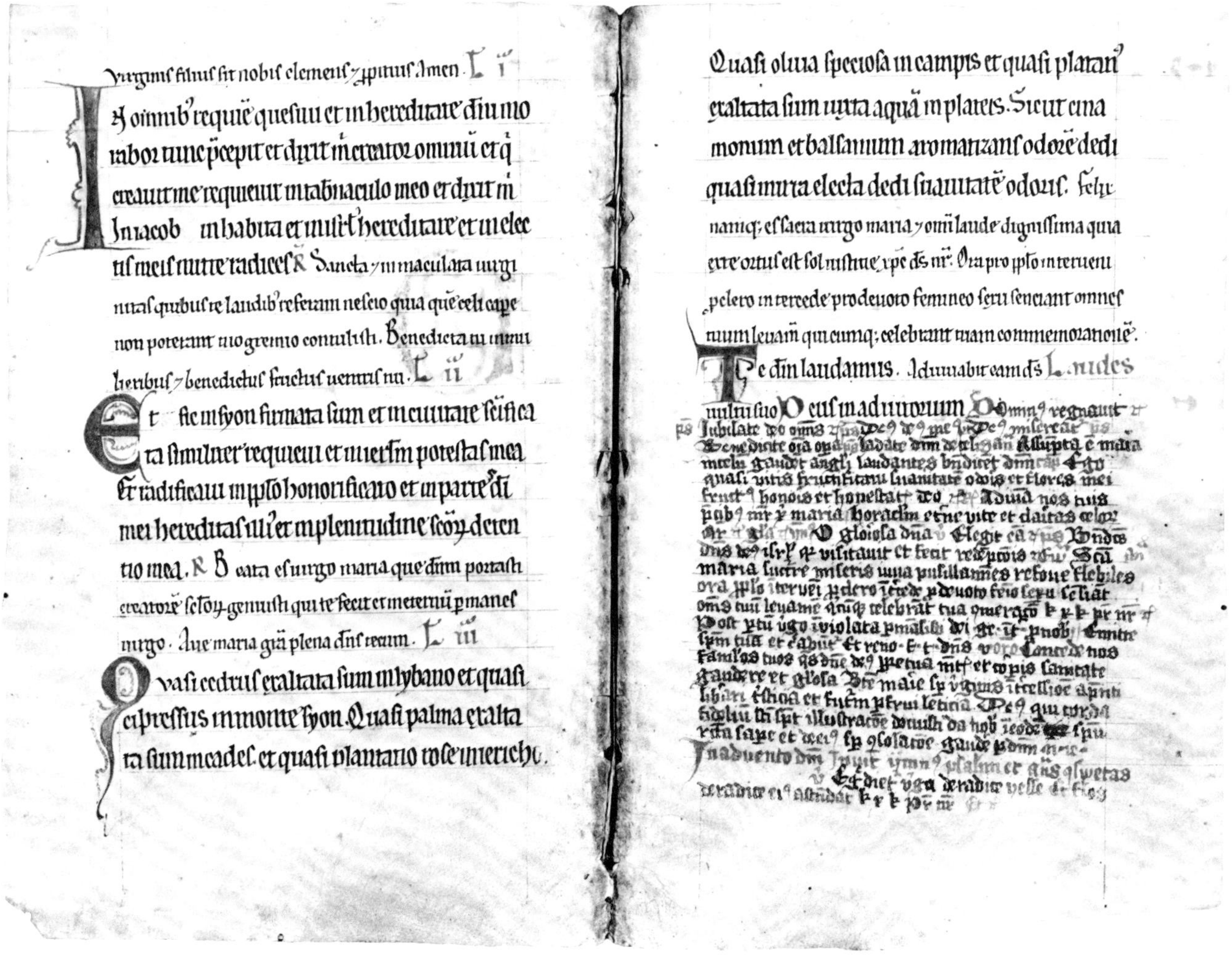

Plate 9. No. 14. MS Lat 282, ff. 26v-27. 3/5 actual size.

hours in brief. They both include very brief scriptural lessons, Psalms and other prayers. Although monastic in origin, they are also found in Psalters intended for lay use. From the end of the twelfth or early thirteenth centuries they are also found in Books of Hours. By the fourteenth and fifteenth centuries, Books of Hours, which survive in countless, often beautifully decorated copies, replaced the Psalter as the main devotional book for the laity.

In the fifteenth century, these leaves were included in a workable, but rather crude manuscript, containing an Office Hymnal for Franciscan Use, a litany, prayers for the dead, and part of the Temporale for the Office.[1] A number of different manuscripts, including the twelfth-century fragment shown here, were used in assembling the volume. The ingenuity and thrift exhibited by the manuscript's fifteenth-century compilers are amply demonstrated by examining one small section, the six leaves taken from a twelfth-century manuscript. Part of the twelfth-century text on these leaves was preserved and part of it was scraped away, so that the parchment could be re-used for different texts.

The Office of the Dead, copied in a twelfth-century hand, now begins near the bottom of the page on f. 23, and continues through f. 25v, where it breaks off abruptly in the ninth lesson at Matins.[2] The remainder of the Office was then scraped away, and rewritten in a very abbreviated fashion by a fifteenth-century scribe, beginning with the response to the ninth lesson. The scribe finished this text at the bottom of f. 25v, and copied a selection of other prayers at the top of f. 26. This same fifteenth-century scribe scraped away the text on the top of f. 23, before the Office of the Dead, and added various other prayers for the Dead.

The Hours of the Virgin, which are written in the same twelfth-century hand as the Office of the Dead, follow the prayers on f. 26, beginning at about the middle of the page. Only the beginning of these devotions — Matins and part of Lauds — was retained by the fifteenth-century scribe, who presumably scraped away the end, and then completed the text of Lauds on f. 27.[3] He did not, however, choose to copy the remaining section of the Hours of the Virgin, and instead began copying the Temporale for the Office at the bottom of f. 27; this section of the manuscript continues through the last twelfth-century leaf, f. 28, and into the final quire, which is assembled from leaves made of fifteenth-century parchment.

BIBLIOGRAPHY: Faye and Bond, 245. FURTHER READING: L. M. J. Delaissé, "The Importance of Books of Hours for the History of the Medieval Book," *Gatherings in Honor of Dorothy E. Miner*, U. E. McCracken, L. M. C. Randall, and R. H. Randall, Jr., eds. (Baltimore 1974) 203-225; Janet Backhouse, *Books of Hours* (London 1985).

NOTES:

[1]Rough outline of the contents of the manuscript as follows: ff. 1-3v, Hymns, from another fifteenth-century manuscript, ending imperfectly; ff. 4-20, Office Hymnal for Franciscan Use; f. 20rv, additional hymns added in another hand; ff. 21-22v, Litany; the contents of ff. 23-28v, the twelfth-century leaves with fifteenth-century interventions, and the concluding fifteenth-century text on ff. 29-32v are discussed below.

[2]Ff. 23-25v Office of the Dead, unidentified use; lessons and responses as follows: 1. Nedes alienis honorem tuum . . ., R. Credo quod redemptor meus vivit . . .; 2. Melius est nomen bonum . . ., R. Qui lazarum resuscitasti . . .; 3.

Memento creatoris tui . . ., R. Peccantem me cotidie . . .; 4. Viuent mortui tui domine . . ., R. Heu michi domine . . .; 5. Hec dicit dominus, de manu mortis liberabo . . ., R. Ne recorderis peccata mea . . .; 6. Multi de his qui dormiunt . . ., R. Domine secundum actum meum . . .; 7. Sicut in adam . . ., R. Redemptor meus uiuit . . .; 8. Ecce misterium . . ., R. Libera mea [corr.[2]: me] domine de uiis inferni . . .; 9. Ipsi fratres diligenter . . ., R. [added in a later hand] Requiem eterna dona et lux . . . .

[3]Ff. 26-27 Hours of the Virgin, unidentified use; Matins with three lessons (In omnibus requiem . . .; Et sic in syon firmata sum . . .; Quasi cedrus exaltata . . .), and Lauds only.

15. Augustine, Commentary on the Psalms, 101–150

Germany (?) s. XII[med]   fMS Typ 703

Parchment (excellent quality, white and even), ff. ii + 178 (modern foliation, very top, outer corner, cited; incorrectly foliated, 1-179, outer margin, near top line of text; foliation, bottom, outer corner, attempts to reconstruct correct order), 465 x 312 (350-345 x 215-211) mm. 2 columns, 52 lines. Ruled very lightly in lead, with the top 2 or 3 and bottom 2 or 3 horizontal rules full across on some folios; single full-length vertical bounding lines. Prickings in all 4 margins.

Too tightly bound for accurate collation, but most quires contain 8 leaves; no catchwords or quire signatures. Misbound: correct order as follows: [leaf missing before f. 1], ff. 1-6, 9-56, [leaf missing following f. 56], 59, 8, 57, 58, 7, 68-156, 60-67, 157-178.

Written on the top line in an even, twelfth-century minuscule; 'et' usually abbreviated by an ampersand (also used internally); straight 's' and 'd' predominate, although round 'd' is also used; 'ae' usually written e-cedilla.

Major initials placed within the text of the commentaries, where the first verse of the Psalm is cited, rather than at the beginning of the commentaries on each Psalm. F. 46v (Psalm 109), 12-line blue initial, with body of initial infilled with heavy knots and interlace patterns in green and orange on a pinkish-purple stepped ground, dotted with white and orange; within the initial is a blue vine, terminating in heavy leaves on pinkish-purple; f. 7 (Psalm 118), 11-line interlace initial, drawn in green and purple outline, infilled with a complicated vine-scroll, with purple used around the outside of the initial to form a partial ground, with the second letter of the psalm entwined within the first. Initials for remaining psalms of varying types: 8- to 12-line interlace initials, in deep blue with black and white used for shading (for example, f. 14, Psalm 103), or in green or reddish-orange outline (for example, f. 38v, Psalm 106); or 7- to 4-line initials in blue, red, green or purple, undecorated or with "arabesque" decoration in contrasting colors. The opening words of the psalm often copied in smaller colored capitals, with red, brown, blue, green and purple intermixed, sometimes placed within the large initial (for example, f. 30, Psalm 104), and often decoratively joined together. Smaller initials, usually undecorated, at the beginning of the commentary on each psalm; 1-line initials used within the text of each commentary. Rubrics in red or purple, or in black with a green line drawn through them for highlighting. Belonged to Chester Beatty; his MS 129; Beatty sale, London, Sotheby's, 24 July 1969, lot 45 (with plate of initials, ff. 46v, 7, and 85). Purchased by Philip Hofer from Bromer, Watertown, Massachusetts, July 16, 1979; Hofer bequest, 1984. Secundo folio (now f. 1): Hoc est exaudi.

AUGUSTINE'S COMMENTARY ON THE PSALMS, which has been known since Erasmus' time as the *Enarrationes in psalmos*, is Augustine's longest work, as well as his most important and influential exegetical treatise.[1] It is also an extremely diverse work, which Augustine assembled from his spoken sermons and from commentaries which were intended from the outset to circulate in written form, composed over a period of many years. The surviving manuscripts indicate that the treatise was especially valued during the twelfth century, when it was considered an essential part of the monastic library.[2] It was usually copied in three volumes during the Middle Ages; our manuscript is possibly the last of such a three-volume set.

The very beautiful — and very large — copy of Augustine's commentary exhibited here is an excellent example of a patristic commentary designed for public reading during the Office at Matins.[3] One could argue quite convincingly that it was intended for this use, simply by pointing to its size. In the case of this manuscript, however, there is no need to guess, since the liturgical lessons are marked in

EXPLICIT PREFATIO.

INCIPIUNT OMELIAE AURELII AUGUSTINI DE PSALMO CENTESIMO XVIII

BEATI IMMACULATI

...in via qui ambulant in lege domini...

Plate 10. No. 15. fMS Typ 703, f. 7. 1/2 actual size.

44

the margins by the numbers 1-3 (for the three lessons in each nocturn) and their opening words. These annotations are in a hand contemporary with the manuscript, and possibly were added by the scribe as he copied the text. The text of the manuscript has been extensively corrected; suggesting that its scribes were either very careless, or using a poor exemplar. These corrections were made by scraping off the original text and rewriting the passage in the blank space. It is also interesting to observe that there are virtually no marginal notes in this manuscript added by contemporary or later readers, although in a few cases the original small numbers for the lessons have been supplemented by more easily spotted red roman numerals. This absence of notes is understandable when the book is seen as one designed for liturgical use; books used for study, in the Middle Ages, as today, frequently contain extensive comments.

No bibliography on this manuscript.

NOTES:

[1]D. Eligius Dekkers, O.S.B. and Iohannes Fripont, eds., in CC 38, 39, 40 (Turnholt 1956); *CPL* 283; Stegmüller 1463.

[2]A. Wilmart, "La tradition," 2:295-315, listing 368

manuscripts; our manuscript not included.

[3]Text begins imperfectly in the commentary on Psalm 101; edition (cited above), p. 1452, sec. 3, line 24.

16. Remigius of Auxerre, On the Celebration of the Mass
Germany s. XII$^{3/4}$ MS Lat 158

Parchment, ff. i + 8 + i, 222-219 x 142-137, unevenly trimmed (183-181 x 108-105) mm. 41 long lines. Ruled in hard point; the horizontal rules extend irregularly past the vertical bounding lines, with some full across; double full-length vertical bounding lines. Prickings in three outer margins (cut away on some folios).

One quire of 8. The text begins and ends imperfectly; originally the third quire of a longer manuscript; signed with a roman numeral, f. 1, bottom margin, right of center.

Written on the top line by one scribe in an informal twelfth-century minuscule, influenced by chancery practice; using round 'd,' and round 's' occasionally, and 'e' for 'ae.' "Qui" is abbreviated in the Italian manner, but the hand exhibits no other Italian characteristics.

Divided into short sections beginning with 2- to 1-line simple initials, brown ink, presumably in the hand of the main scribe, placed within the written space; decoration confined to dots on the initial and elaboration of the letter form, for example, 'S' is elongated and copied on its side. Majuscules within the text stroked with red, ff. 1 and 8v. Purchased January 18, 1937, from Erik von Scherling (Treat Fund). Secundo folio: [huius]modi uoce laudacionis.

THE CONTENT OF REMIGIUS of Auxerre's (c. 841-c. 908), *De celebratione missae,*[1] differs from what a modern reader might expect from the title. It is not a manual on how to say the Mass, nor is it an examination of the historical development of the liturgy, or a theoretical treatise discussing the place of the Mass in the life of the Church or individual believer. This short treatise can probably be best understood as a commentary on the text of the Mass. Remigius himself was the author of biblical commentaries, and his methods here are similar to those found in medieval commentaries on the Bible.[2]

After a short introductory section discussing why the Mass is celebrated, and why it is called the Mass, or *Missa,* Remigius analyzes its structure and content by proceeding through the text step by step, explaining the origins of the words, and commenting on the significance of the liturgical practices. He often stresses the scriptural authority behind the phrases used. For example, he notes that the use of the phrase, "Dominus vobiscum" ("The Lord be with you"), is founded on the Christ's promise to his disciples, "Ecce ego vobiscum sum [Matthew 28:20]" ("And look, I am with you always"), and echoed in numerous other biblical passages, including Gabriel's promise to Mary, "Ave, gratia plena, Dominus tecum [Luke 1:28]" ("Rejoice, you who enjoy God's favour), and Booz's salutation to the reapers, "Dominus vobiscum [Ruth 2:4]" ("The Lord be with you").[3] His discussion of the reading of the Gospels during Mass includes an examination of why the deacon stands during the reading, why he faces in a certain direction, and why he makes the sign of the cross in preparation for the reading.[4]

Remigius focusses on explaining the text; his purpose is not one of exhortation. Nonetheless, he allows himself to show some emotion in the short passage which explains the meaning of "Evangelium," or "Gospel":

> After this, the Gospel follows, which is taken from the Greek and means in Latin, the good news. And what could be better news, than that, "Repent, for the Kingdom of Heaven is close at hand [Matthew 3:2]," which in the Gospel refers to the Incarnation of the Son of God, and to His miracles, His preaching, and to His resurrection, and ascension, and to the glory of the elect, and the damnation of the reprobate.[5]

Remigius' commentary circulated as part of a longer treatise by an unknown author, known as *De divinis officiis,* once ascribed to Alcuin. The text of our manuscript, which consists of only eight folios, is incomplete at the beginning and end, and it is possible that it once formed part of a larger manuscript containing the complete Ps-Alcuinian text.[6] The small format of this very plain and functional manuscript designed for study, stands in sharp contrast to the much grander public copy of Augustine's *Commentary on the Psalms,* also in this case (see cat. no. 15).

BIBLIOGRAPHY: Faye and Bond, 237.

NOTES:

[1]Printed in *PL* 101:1246-1271, as chapter 40 of Ps-Alcuin, *Liber de divinis officiis*, col. 1173-1286; see M. Manitius, *Geschichte der lateinischen Literatur des Mittelalters.* Handbuch der klassischen Altertumswissenschaft, ed. I. von Müller, 9, Abt. 2 (1911-31) 1:504-19, with addenda, 2:808 and 3:1063, and *Lexikon für Theologie und Kirche,* M. Buchberger, ed. (10 vols., 1930-1938) 8:1224. We thank Professor R. H. Rouse for his comments on the date and origin of this manuscript, April, 1987.

[2]See Smalley, *Study of the Bible,* 40-41; and A. Vaccari, "Il genuino commeto ai Salmi di Remigio di Auxerre," *Biblica* 26 (1945) 52-99.

[3]*PL* 101:1248B; biblical citations in English are from *The New Jerusalem Bible.*

[4]*PL* 101:1250B.

[5]*PL* 1251B: "Hinc sequitur Evangelium, quod de Graeco in Latinum, sonat bonum nuntium. Et quod est melius nuntium, quam istud: Poenitentiam agite, appropinquabit enim regnum caelorum [Matthew 3:2]; quae in Evangelio dicuntur de Incarnatione Filii Dei, et de eius miraculis, praedicatione, et resurrectione, atque ascensione, de gloria quoque electorum, et damnatione reproborum?" Cf. MS Lat 158, f. 2v.

[6]Here beginning and ending imperfectly, *PL* 101:1248C-1265D, as follows: ff. 1-8v "//streque martirum duxit, instituit ut hymnicus anglicus diceretur hoc est gloria in excelsis deo ante sacrificium . . . [f. 1, line 4] Postea dicit sacerdos dominus uobiscum salutans populum et orans . . . iuxta quod ipse dicit, 'Sancti estote quoniam sanctus sum dominus deus uester [1 Peter 1:16].' Primum fuit deus omnipotens//" Although the manuscript generally seems to agree with the printed text, the wording of the opening section discussing the hymn, "Gloria in excelsis," differs significantly.

TWO COPIES OF THE CONFESSIONS OF ST. AUGUSTINE

17. Augustine, Confessions[1]
Italy (?) s. XII^2/4   MS Lat 150

Parchment, ff. 111 + i, 243 x 185 (200-197 x 146-140) mm. 29-28 long lines. Ruled lightly in hard point with the top 3 and bottom 4 horizontal rules full across on some folios; full-length double vertical bounding lines. Prickings in outer and bottom margins.

1-2^8 3^8 (3, f. 19, and 6, f. 22, are single) 4^8 5^8 (3, f. 35, and 6, f. 38, are single) 6-10^8 11^8 (3, f. 83, and 6, f. 86, are single) 12-13^8 14^8 (-8, following f. 111, cancelled with no loss of text).

Written on the top line in a twelfth-century minuscule; round 'd' used occasionally; 'ae' written 'e'; the scribe avoids carrying words over two pages by finishing words below the written space under the last word on the page.

Book begins with 8- to 4-line initials, drawn in outline in brown ink with acanthus-motifs used to form the initial or entwined around it, infilled or outlined in red-orange; book 10, f. 64v, begins with a 'C' in the form of a wolf. Headings for each book in freely formed red rustic capitals, highlighted in pale yellow wash; yellow lines drawn through the rubrics for highlighting; explicits and opening words of most books in similar rustics in black daubed with red. Belonged to John B. Stetson; his gift to the library, December 11, 1935. Secundo folio: hanc et apprehendam.

BIBLIOGRAPHY: De Ricci, 2303.

18. Augustine, Confessions
Northern Italy (?) s. XII^med   MS Richardson 27

Parchment (hair side yellowed), ff. i + 85 + ii, 271 x 182 mm., trimmed; cf. f. 1, top of initial cut away; (211-199 x 125-120) mm. 34-33 long lines. Ruled in hard point with the top 3 and bottom 3 horizontal rules full across; single full-length vertical bounding lines. Some prickings, outer margin.

1-2^8 3^8(-4, following f. 23v, with loss of text) 4-10^8 11^8 (-7, 8, following f. 85, cancelled with no loss of text). Quires signed in small roman numerals, middle, bottom margin, verso of last leaf (cut away in quires 9 and 10).

Written above the top line in a twelfth-century minuscule; 'ae' usually written e-cedilla, but use is not consistent.

F. 1, 8-line very dark blue initial infilled with gold and red decorative motifs and small white leaves. Remaining books begin with 9- to 5-line red initials (with extensions up to 11-lines) with decorative void spaces within the initials, decorated with acanthus leaves and other vegetal motifs, drawn as part of the initial in red, or occasionally, brown ink, with highlights in yellow wash; initial f. 44 is brown; initials on ff. 14 and 19v are similar to those used in manuscripts from Morimondo (cf. fMS Typ 223, cat. no. 10). Red rubrics in fanciful capitals; opening words of text in capitals modelled on rustics. Belonged to William King Richardson; Richardson bequest, March 1, 1951. Accession record: *50M-281. Secundo folio: tecum qui ueritas.

BIBLIOGRAPHY: De Ricci, 2300 (= Boston, library of W. K. Richardson, MS 27); cf. Faye and Bond, 246.

OF ALL THE MEDIEVAL and patristic works represented in this exhibition, the *Confessions* of St. Augustine is probably the one most frequently read today by a broad audience.[2] It was also an extremely influential and popular work throughout the Middle Ages. The distribution of the surviving manuscripts indicates, moreover, that this treatise is an example of a patristic text which was valued equally by the monks of the twelfth century, by the scholastics of the thirteenth and fourteenth centuries and by the new book collectors and scholars of the Renaissance.[3] The *Confessions* is not, strictly speaking, a commentary on the Bible, although the usual modern description of the work as an autobiography is almost equally misleading. Augustine's chief aim was to praise God for His grace, especially as it was manifested in the Saint's own conversion, recounted in the first ten books, and in the creation, told in the remaining three. In part, these last three books are a commentary on the beginning of Genesis, expressed in a manner which almost makes them an extended prayer or hymn. Augustine's language and style, which owes much to the Bible as well as to late Antique rhetorical conventions, influenced the monastic authors of the Middle Ages. His love of the Bible, expressed movingly in the *Confessions*, was an equally important part of his bequest to the Middle Ages.

The layout in both of these copies of the *Confessions* is similar. Both are simply divided into the usual thirteen books, and both include marginal notes. Those in MS Lat 150 were added by readers during the twelfth and thirteenth centuries in

nõ aдtr custodiebi. Sz pfeecussti abste inregione longinqua. ut ea dissipare in
meretrices cupiditates. Na qd in pderat bonares nõ utenta bene. Noeni sen
ciebi illas artes & ta abstudiosis & ingeniosis difficillime intelligi. nisi cu eis easde
conabar exponere. & erat ille excellentissim' meis. q̃ne exponente nocardi seque
retur. Sz qd in hoc pderat putarit qd tu dne dsi ueritas corp' ces lucidu & immi
si. tego frustu de illo corpore. samia puerstas. Sz siceri. No erubesco dne dsi
nis cõfiteri te inne misedias tuas & quuocarete. qui noerubui tunc pfiteri homi
nib; blasphemias meis. iluatrare aduersu te. Qd idq̃ nr tunc pderat ingeniu p illa
doctrinas agile & nullo amminiculo humani magisterii tot nodosissim libri
enodata. cu deformiti insacrilega turpidine indoctrina pietatis errart. Aut
qd tantu oberat paruulis tuis longe tardi ingenii cu mate longe nõ recedeti.
ut inmdo ecclesie tue tuti plumescerent. & alas caritatis almtco sane fidi nutri
rent. Odie ds nr muelancio alaru tuaru spes. & pregus. importas tos. Tu
portabis iparuulos. & usq; adcanos tu portabis qin firmitas nra quando tua
est tunc e firmitas. cu aute nra e infirmitas. Viuit apud te sep bonu nrm &
quia puersi sum'. inde auersi simi. Reuertamur ia dne. ut nõ euertamur. qz uiuit
apudte sine ullo affectu bonu nrm qd tu ipse es. & notunebim nequisit quore
deamus. qz nos inde ruim'. Nob aut absentib; nõ ruit domi nra. eternitas tua.

Explicit lib. III. INCIPIT LIBER IIII.
ACCEPE SACRIFICIVM CONFES
SIONV MEARV. DE MANV LINGVE MEE QVAM
formasti & excitasti. ut cõfiteat nomini tuo. sa
na omia ossa mea & dicant. dne qs similis tibi.
Neq; eni docet te qd insc agat qt cõfiteat. qz
oculu tuu nõ excludit cor clausu. nec manu tua
repellit duricia hominu. sz soluis ea cu uoles aut
miserans aut uindicans. & nõe qz se abscõdat acalore tuo. Sz te laudet ani
ma mea ut amet te. & cõfiteat tibi miseraciones tuas ut laudet te. Nõ ces
sat nec tacet laudes tuas uniuersa creatura tua. nec sps omis p os cõuer sum
adte. nec animalia nec corporalia p os cõsideranciu ea. ut exurgat inre alas
situdine anima nra. innitens eis que fecisti. transiens adte q̃ fecisti hec mi
rabilit. & ibi refectio & uera fortitudo. Eant & fugiant ate inquieti & iniq̃.
& tu uides eos. & distinguis umbras. & ecce pulcra tt cu eis omia. & ipsi turpes tt.

Plate 11. No. 18. MS Richardson 27, f. 19v. 4/5 actual size.

49

informal scripts, and are an interesting reflection of what certain readers found most noteworthy in the contents of the text. For example, a twelfth-century reader wrote on f. 24: "Note the marvelous talent of Augustine" ("Nota mirabile ingenium augustini"). A thirteenth-century reader was most interested in "exempla," that is, passages in the text containing anecdotes that usefully illustrated a moral point; on f. 51, this reader notes that there is an "exemplum" about St. Anthony. The notes in MS Richardson 27 are more formal. They are written in a very small, precise twelfth-century script, and are usually surrounded by a box drawn in brown ink. Most of these notes function as guides to the contents. On f. 6v, for example, the note informs the reader that Augustine is describing thefts he committed when he was a boy, and on f. 13v, that he is recounting his mother's dream.

In MS Lat 150, the headings for each book of the *Confessions* were copied in red; red was also used to highlight the opening and closing words of each book. The use of color and different styles of script to emphasize the beginnings of new sections of a text was a common practice; it can be seen in most of the manuscripts included in this exhibition. In this manuscript, however, red was also used in a more idiosyncratic manner. Red is used to highlight the majuscules on the first page of each book, or on the double-paged opening with an initial. It is also used to fill in spaces left by the scribe because of defects in the parchment (for example, f. 95rv), and to indicate that the scribe has completed a word on the beginning of the next line, or above or below the line; when red is used for such a purpose the majuscules in the text on that page are usually also filled in with red. The use of red in this manner indicates that it was added after the manuscript was completed, either by the scribe or another member of the scriptorium. It seems likely that it was not routinely done as part of the decoration, but was rather the final step in the production of the text, which included at least superficial proof-reading.

FURTHER READING: The *Confessions* have been translated into English many times; one translation is by Edward B. Pusey, *The Confessions of Saint Augustine* (New York 1961); one of the best modern biographies of Augustine is Peter Brown, *Augustine of Hippo: A Biography* (London 1967).

NOTES:

[1]The manuscript has traditionally been ascribed to Italy; the script and decoration, however, suggest that it might have been copied in Germany, in an area where Italian influence was strong.

[2]Martinus Skulltella, ed. (Leipzig 1934[1]), revised by H. Juergens and W. Schaub (Stuttgart 1969); *CPL* 251; text in MS Richardson 27 is imperfect: one folio missing following f. 23v; f. 23v ends imperfectly ". . . Metuebam itaque credere in carne natum // [book 5:10; ed., p. 93, line 30]"; f. 24 begins abruptly, "//mihi apparentibus commedata, do-

2]"; outer margin, f. 85, partly cut or torn away, with loss of text at the end of the lines (book 13:32-38; cf. ed., p. 369, line 17-p. 371, end).

[3]Wilmart, "La tradition," 2:261; Wilmart lists 258 manuscripts of the *Confessions*, 52 of which date from the twelfth century, 51 from the thirteenth, 46 from the fourteenth, and 70 from the fifteenth, see pp. 259-266; MS Lat 150 is listed on p. 262 (no. 46, as Cheltenham, ex-Phillipps, MS 9460). MS Richardson 27 is not included in his list.

19. Gregory the Great, Moralia in Job, books 26-35
Italy (Morimondo) s. XII² fMS Typ 702

Parchment (fairly stiff), ff. i + 52 + i, 408 x 269 (320-317 x 196-194) mm. 2 columns, 39 lines. Ruled in lead with some horizontal rules extending irregularly past the vertical bounding lines; full-length vertical bounding lines, single on the far inside and outside, and triple between the columns. Pricked in all 4 margins, with double prickings in the outer margin aligned with the penultimate line.

1-19⁸. Horizontal catchwords, inside margin, near bottom edge; quires are signed in roman numerals, usually decorated on 4 sides with dots or other flourishes, lower margin, verso of last leaf of quire (location varies).

Written above the top line by a number of scribes; the first scribe copied f. 1, lines 1-6, in a clear, angular, twelfth-century minuscule; the remaining hands are more rounded; letter unions (except 'pp') are avoided; e-cedilla is sporadically used for 'ae.'

One 16-line parted red and yellow-wash initial with simple "shadow"-type pen decoration, infilled with red pen strokes, f. 1, book 26. Remaining books begin with 9- to 6-line red initials, often with decorative void spaces, yellow wash and "shadow"-type pen decoration and cross-hatching in red. Red majuscule letters used for the opening letters following the initials, ff. 1 and 143; red rubrics. Majuscules within the text touched with yellow. Guide notes for rubricator, outer margin, f. 99v. Belonged to Philip Hofer; Hofer bequest, 1984. Secundo folio: michi. Dedignatus uidelicet.

BIBLIOGRAPHY: De Ricci, 1696 (= New York, Collection of Philip Hofer, MS 18).

20. Gregory the Great, Moralia in Job, books 23-29
Belgium (Meuse valley) or Germany (?) s. XII³/⁴ MS Lat 167

Parchment (smooth and uniform), ff. ii + 119 + ii, 283 x 194 mm. Layout varies from (219-217 x 160-155) mm., in 2 columns, 32 lines, to (237-235 x 157-153) mm., in 2 columns, 34 lines. Ruled in lead with the top, third, third from bottom and bottom horizontal rules full across, except ff. 81-102v, with the top 2, middle 1, and bottom 2 horizontal rules full across; throughout, horizontal rules are not drawn between the two columns, except in the case of those extending full across the page; single full-length vertical bounding lines throughout, except ff. 103v-119, with triple full-length vertical bounding lines between the columns. Prickings, top and bottom margins, most folios; some folios with prickings in the inner margin (cf. ff. 32-72v).

1-9⁸ 10⁶ 11-14⁸ 15⁶ 16³ (structure uncertain; 1 and 2, conjugate pair; no loss of text). Quires signed in roman numerals, decoratively boxed and flourished in red and brown, verso of last leaf of the quire, in the lower margin between the two columns.

Written on the top line in a twelfth-century minuscule by several scribes; 'ae' written e-cedilla; occasional use of round 'r,' 'd' and 's.'

Six 11- to 7-line maroon and green parted initials at the beginning of books with "arabesque" pen-decoration in blue, green and orange, highlighted with pale yellow wash. 15-line interlace "I" at the beginning of book 25, f. 31, in red ink, with the shaft partially infilled with green and blue, and terminating in an animal head with acanthus leaves. Biblical quotations begin with 1-line orange-red or green initials, and are marked in the margins. Opening words following large initials of some books copied in display capitals in blue, orange and green. Majuscules in text stroked with red (except f. 16, pale yellow). Guide letters for initials in a minute, formal hand. Presented to the library in 1946 by Dr. William Inglis Morse. Secundo folio: unam personam.

BIBLIOGRAPHY: Faye and Bond, 238.

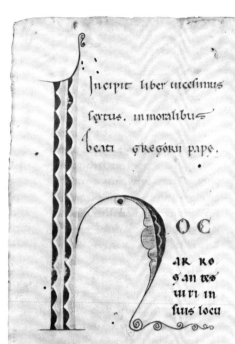

Incipit liber tricesimus
sextus. in moralibus
beati gregorii pape.

O C
AR RO
GAN TES
UI TI IN
SUIS LOCU

tionib; habere inter alia proprium
solent: qd auditoribus suis ne quid for
tasse inordinatum dixerint: tunc requi
cum se laudabilit aliquid dixisse co
gnoscunt. Hoc uidelicet faciunt no
quo de dictis suis ambigant: set quo
audientium iudicio fauores querant.
Nam inueniri facile poterunt. quia a
nimo peiunctant: si quisquam cum eorum
bona laudat: etiam mala rephendat.
Certum quippe e. quia sicut inflant
laudib; ita correptionib; inflamant.
et a quolibet se l iuste rephendi despi
tiunt: in eorz in suis malis fomite de
fensionis exquirunt. Quom ergo de
bonis suis humiliat ambigunt: qui
mala sua etia puerse defende mo li
untur: Ille e enim uere humilis i boī:
qui non e defensor i malis. Nam qui de
malis suis arguit: contra uerba argueti
accenduntur: qn de bonis suis quasi hu

militer turba psa militaris uoce or
nari appetit ñ docet. Helui uacp uita
arrogantium signant: pquam multa inia
et sublimia intulit: ecce in ubis forma
humilitatis assumit: requitate pposita
sub quada disciplatus imagine beatu
iob alloquit dicens. Quia ego loquutur
sū ad deum te quoqp non prohibeo. Si er
mur tu doce me: si iniquitatem locutus
ultra ñ addam. Sicut sepe contingit.
ut bona 7 mali loquant: multa helui
fortia paulo supi se dixisse meminerat
et securus dico ne fortasse errauit requisut.
Neqp enim requireret: si se errasse credidis
set. Enamqp ut dixi pa arroganti fia
ut requirere de errore studeant: qui se
nouerint ñ errasse. Quia rursu requirere l
argui de errore despitiunt: si qui se errasse
se ueraci pcognoscunt. Nõ eū qd ti uidi
humiles appetunt: et ti requirendo spe tie
humilitatis assumunt: qui de ipsa magis
requisitoe laudant. Set quia omino
difficile e. ut clario qregnat i corde. no
erumpat in uoce: auditores arrogantiu
si eorz dicta paulisp tacit expectant: atp
considerant: eicuis corda illoz subse
quentia uba manifestant. Uiri qppe mo
tari ñ possunt: in ipsa humilitatis imagi
ne: qua spetetenus sumunt. Sub psen
tib; humilitas alta e: i cum ei formam
consciende ambiunt: lassant ai gressib;
quasi ac huosis atqp aspis itineribus de
labuntur. Alienum e salicet quod uidi
appetunt: i idcirco ei imagini inherere
diu nequaqua possunt. Graue pondus
erumant: cum eam salut spetetenus por
tant: i quousqp bane abitiant ui qua
dam i corde patiunt: quia uidelicet
dationis usu male diuinam deseruiunt

Plate 12. No. 19. fMS Typ 702, f. 1. 1/2 actual size.

52

THE *Moralia in Job*, by GREGORY THE GREAT (c. 540-604) was one of the most frequently copied biblical commentaries during the Middle Ages.[1] Like Augustine's *Enarrationes in Psalmos* (see cat. no. 15), the *Moralia* was a text which was owned by most twelfth-century monasteries. In his dedicatory epistle to Leander, Bishop of Seville, Gregory explains that the work originated as a series of talks given at the request of the monks who accompanied him to Constantinople during the years, c. 579 — 586. He revised these talks into book form in the period between his return to Rome and his election as Pope in 590. Gregory's Commentary on the book of Job, like most other patristic and medieval commentaries, does not focus on the literal, or historical, sense of the text. He is more interested in seeking the hidden meanings of the text, by exploring the "typical," or allegorical, and moral interpretations. He comments on this approach in his prologue:

> But be it known that there are some parts, which we go through in a historical exposition, some we trace out in allegory upon an investigation of the typical meaning, some we open in the lessons of moral teaching alone, allegorically conveyed, while there are some few which, with more particular care, we search out in all these ways together, exploring them in a threefold method. For first, we lay the historical foundations; next, by pursuing the typical sense, we erect a fabric of the mind to be a strong hold of faith; and moreover, as the last step, by the grace of moral understanding, we, as it were, clothe the edifice with an overcast of coloring.[2]

fMS Typ 702 is a handsome, large-format copy of this popular text, which was copied at the Cistercian Abbey of Morimondo in Italy. The sixth item listed in the late twelfth-century library catalogue from Morimondo (see cat. nos. 1 and 10), is a copy of the *Moralia* in two volumes: "Moralia in Iob in duobus uoluminibus." Traditionally, this entry has been accepted as a description of our manuscript.[3] An examination of how the *Moralia* was copied during the Middle Ages, however, raises some doubt as to the validity of this assertion.

The *Moralia* was a very lengthy treatise, divided into thirty-five books. Gregory's prefaces indicate that he intended it to be copied in six volumes, with divisions at books 6, 11, 17, 23 and 28. Medieval scribes did not always follow this schema, and they experimented with two-, three- and four-volume formats for the *Moralia*; in the thirteenth century and later, one volume copies were occasionally produced. The usual division for a two-volume copy was after book 16; some scribes broke from Gregory's divisions and divided their text after books 17 or 18.[4] fMS Typ 702 includes books 26-35 of Gregory's Commentary. If it were the second of a two-volume copy of the complete *Moralia*, the first volume would have had to include books 1-25. Such a division seems unlikely, since the two volumes would have been very unequal in size. One can think of hypothetical solutions to this problem. For example, it is possible that the copy of the *Moralia* mentioned in Morimondo's catalogue was the first two volumes of a three-volume set, which was not yet complete when the catalogue was compiled. The identification of our manuscript with the third volume of this copy would raise no problems. At this time such an interpretation is purely conjectural. Nonetheless, even if our manuscript is not included in Morimondo's library catalogue, its decoration, binding, and modern provenance, point strongly to the fact that it was copied at Morimondo.[5]

MS Lat 167, the other copy of the *Moralia* shown here, includes books 23-29. The text in this manuscript is presented to the reader in a fairly simple fashion. The beginning of each new book is marked by a large, colored initial. The opening words of the text following these initials are copied in colorful display capitals. Citations from Job are marked by one-line red initials within the text, and the customary small marks in the margin that resemble modern quotation marks. In common with most twelfth-century copies of this text, this is a difficult book to use if you are trying to look up a specific passage. The large size of many of the surviving copies, like the copy from Morimondo, fMS Typ 702, suggests they were used for reading at meals and during the Office. MS Lat 167 is smaller than most copies, and was perhaps used as a book for study as well, an hypothesis supported by the numerous *nota* marks added by contemporary hands in the margins.

FURTHER READING: Neil R. Ker, "The English Manuscripts of the Moralia of Gregory the Great," *Kunsthistorische Forschungen; Otto Pächt, zu seinem 70. Geburtstag*, A. Rosenauer and G. Weber, eds. (Salzburg 1972) 77-89; R. Wasselynck, "L'influence de l'éxègese de S. Grégoire le Grand sur les commentaires bibliques médiévaux," *Recherches de théologie ancienne et médiévale* 32 (1965) 157-204; there have been a number of translations of the *Moralia*, among them: Gregory the Great, *Morals on the Book of Job*, translated by Members of the English Church. A Library of Fathers of the Holy Catholic Church Anterior to the Division of the East and West (Oxford 1884); and Grégoire le Grand, *Morales sur Job, troisième partie (livres XI-XVI), texte latin, introduction et notes,* by Astride Bocognano. Sources Chrétiennes 212 (Paris 1974).

NOTES:

[1]Edited by Marcus Adriaen in CC 143, 143A and 143B (Turnholt, Belgium 1979-1985), listing fMS Typ 702 on p. xxiii (as Hofer MS 18) and MS Lat 167 on p. xviii of vol. 143; *CPL* 1708; Stegmüller 2634.

[2]Edition, cited above, vol. 143, p. 4, lines 106-114; English translation from Gregory the Great, *Morals on the Book of Job*, translated by Members of the English Church. A Library of Fathers of the Holy Catholic Church Anterior to the Division of the East and West (Oxford 1884), 7.

[3]Leclercq, "Manuscrits cisterciens," 177; two copies of the *Moralia* are listed in the eighteenth-century catalogue of Morimondo in Vatican City, Biblioteca Apostolica Vaticana, MS Barberini 3229, also printed by Leclercq, 181-2, nec aliquid certi eluceret . . . [book 5:14; ed., p. 98, line

nos. 7 and 28.

[4]See N. R. Ker, "The English Manuscripts of the Moralia of Gregory the Great," *Kunsthistorische Forschungen: Otto Pächt, zu seinem 70. Geburtstag*, A. Rosenauer and G. Weber, eds. (Salzburg 1972) 81.

[5]The initial shown in M. R. James, *A Descriptive Catalogue of the McClean Collection of Manuscripts in the Fitzwilliam Museum* (Cambridge 1912) plate LXXV, reproducing f. 41v of McClean MS 116 (Origen, On the Old Testament), may be compared with the initials in fMS Typ 702. As noted above (see cat. no. 1), the opening lines of fMS Typ 702 are copied in an angular script similar to the script in the McClean manuscript; the remainder of the manuscript was copied by scribes using rounder hands.

negligent admisisset. Quia ergo unumquemque; electum suum diuina gratia tum magis erudiendo custodit. cum quasi percutiens deserit. dicat recte. appropinquauit
corruptioni anima eius. et uita illi mortiferis. Et quo se suis uiribus uicinum
morti peraduisa considat. eo in cunctis
que fortiter egerit. ad diuine spei munimen fugiens. solidius uiuat.

Explicit lib. xxiii.
Incipit lib. xxiiii.

ELU VIM
supne dispensationis
insinuans. de electi
uniuscuiusque; percussione intulit dicens.
Appropinquauit corruptioni anima eius.
et uita illi mortiferis. Et dum temptatum
hominem demonstrat unum in qua temptatione sit positum humanum genus
ostendit uniuersum. Duque; narrat
quod specialiter agat in singulis. liquido
intimat quod generaliter agat in cunctis.
Sic enim temptatione expressit quorundam ipse
singulos. ut possit intelligi et uniuersalis omnium. Cunctum quippe electorum
genus in hac uita huius taedio laboris afficitur. Vnde et mox huic generali
pestilentie. generale submittit remedium medicine dicens. Si fuerit pro eo
angelus loquens unum de similibus. ut

annuntiet hominis equitatem. miserebitur eius. Quis enim iste est angelus? nisi
ille qui propheta dicitur. magni consilii
angelus? Quia enim greca lingua euanglizare denuntiare dicitur. semet ipsum
nobis annuntians dominus angelus uocatur.
Et bene ait si fuerit pro eo angelus loquens
quia sicut ait apostolus. etiam interpellat pro
nobis. Sed quia pro nobis loquatur audiam.
Vnum de similibus. Mos medicine est ut
aliquando similia similibus. aliquando contraria contrariis curet. Nam sepe calida calidis. sepe autem frigida calidis.
calida frigidis sanare consueuit. Veniens ergo ad nos desuper medicus nostantis quia nos inueniens languoribus
pressos. quiddam nobis simile. et quiddam contrarium apposuit. Ad homines quippe
homo uenit. sed ad peccatores iustus.
Concordauit nobis ueritate nature. sed
discrepauit a nobis uigore iustitie. Viciosus enim homo corrigi non poterat. non
per dominum. Videri autem debuit qui corrigebat.
ut praebendo imitationis formam ante acte
malitie mutaret uitam. Sed uideri ab homine non poterat deus. Homo ergo factus est.
ut uideri potuisset. Iustus ergo atque; inuisibilis deus apparuit. similis nobis homo
uisibilis. ut dum uidetur ex simili. curaret ex iusto. Et dum ueritate generis
concordat conditioni. uirtute arceret obuiaret egritudinem. Quia ergo in carne
ueniens dominus. non culpam nostram sed uicio.

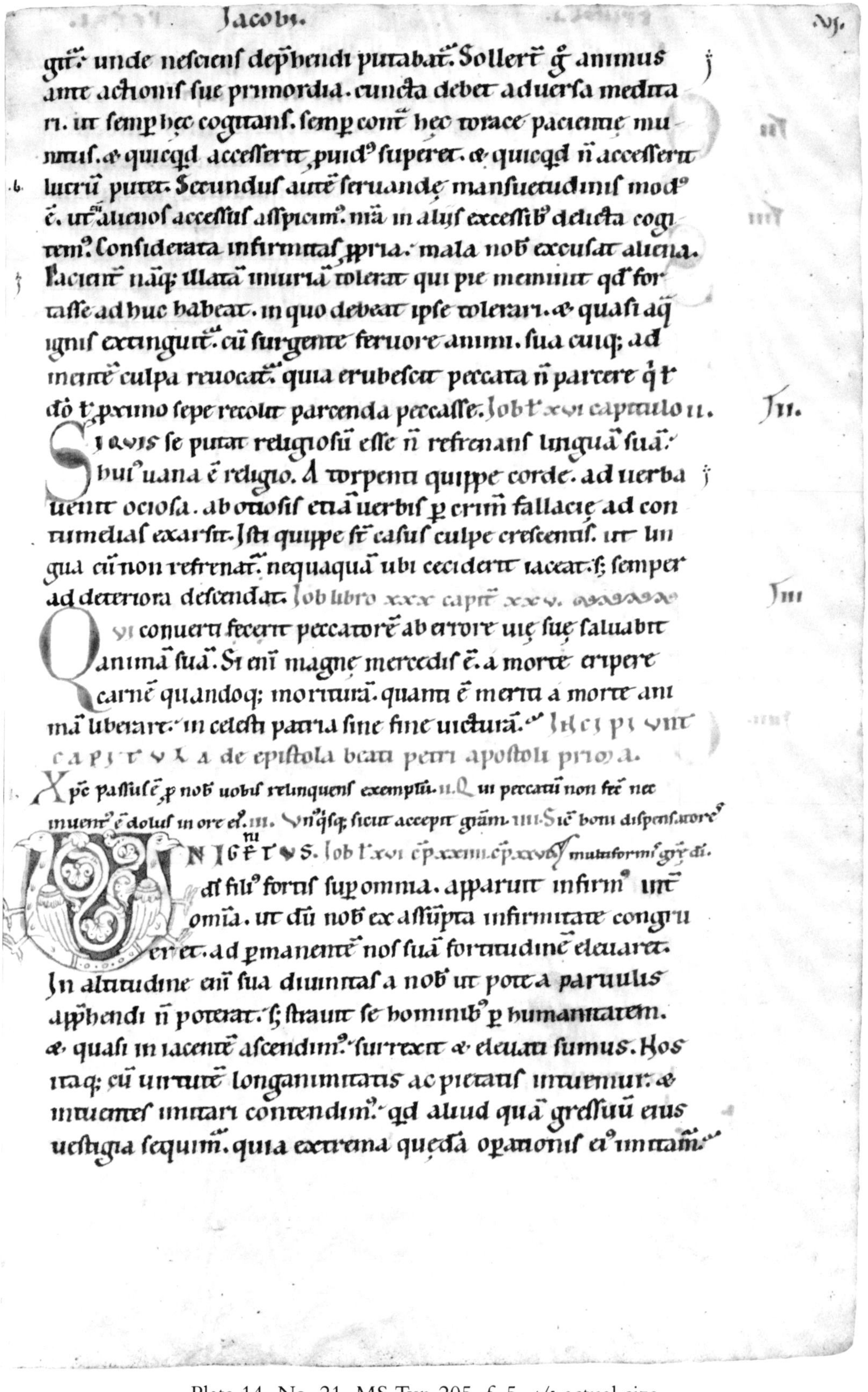

gñr. unde nesciens depħendi putabať. Sollerť ĝ animus
ante actionis sue primordia. cuncta debet aduersa medita
ri. ut semp ħec cogitans. semp cont ħec torace paciente mu
nitus. ø quicqd accesserit, puid⁹ superet. ø quicqd ñ accesserit
lucrū putet. Secundus aute seruande mansuetudinis mod⁹
ē. ut alienos accessus aspiciam. nia in alijs excessib⁹ delicta cogi
tem⁹. Considerata infirmitas ppria. mala nob excusat aliena.
Pacient naqᶻ illata iniuriā tolerat qui pie meminit qd for
tasse ad ħuc ħabeat. in quo debeat ipse tolerari. ø quasi aq̇
ignis extinguiť. cū surgente feruore animi. sua cuiqᶻ ad
mente culpa reuocať. quia erubescat peccata ñ partere q̇ t
dō t pximo sepe recolit parcenda peccasse. Iob t xvi capitulo ii.

SI quis se putat religiosū esse ñ refrenans linguā suā.
ħui⁹ uana ē religio. A torpenti quippe corde. ad uerba
uenit ociosa. ab ociosis etiā uerbis p crim fallacie ad con
tumelias exarsit. Ista quippe sť casus culpe crescentis. ut lin
gua cū non refrenať. nequaquā ubi ceciderit iaceat. sᵉᵈ semper
ad deteriora descendat. Iob libro xxx capit xxv.

QVi conuerti fecerit peccatore ab errore uie sue saluabit
animā suā. Si eni magne mercedis ē. a morte eripere
carne quandoqᶻ morituā. quanti ē meriti a morte ani
mā liberare. in celesti patria sine fine uicturā. INCIPIT
CAPITVLA de epistola beati petri apostoli priora.

Xpē passus ē p nob uobis relinquens exemplū. ii. Q̇ in peccatū non fᵉ nec
inuent⁹ ē dolus in ore ei. iii. Vñiᵃqᶻ sicut accepit grām. iiii. Sic boni dispensatores
NIGET VS. Iob t xvi cp xxiii. cp xxvi⁹ multiformis gr̃e di.
dī fili⁹ fortis sup omnia. apparuit infirm⁹ inf
omnia. ut dū nob ex assūpta infirmitate congru
eret. ad pmanente nos sua fortitudine eleuaret.
In altitudine eni sua diuinitas a nob ut pote a paruulis
apphendi ñ poterat. sᵉᵈ strauit se hominib⁹ p humanitatem.
ø quasi in iacente ascendim⁹. surrexit ø eleuati sumus. Hos
itaqᶻ cū uirtute longanimitatis ac pietatis intuemur. ø
intuentes imitari contendim⁹. qd aliud quā gressuū eius
uestigia sequim⁹. quia externa quedā opationis eⁱ imitam⁹·

Plate 14. No. 21. MS Typ 205, f. 5. 4/5 actual size.

56

21. Bruno, New Testament Commentary compiled from the works of Gregory the Great

Belgium or Germany s. XII^med-3/4   MS Typ 205

Parchment, ff. 96 (medieval foliation added in an early hand in roman numerals, top, outer corner recto through f. 47 [now f. 46]), 266 x 175 mm. Layout varies, quire 1, ff. 1-8v, (218-214 x 124) mm. 35 long lines; ff. 9-end, (210-205 x 120) mm. 30-31 long lines (except f. 9, with an extra line). Ruled in lead, usually with the top 2 and bottom 2 horizontal rules full across; single full-length vertical bounding lines. Prickings in three outer margins.

1⁸ (-1, with loss of text) 2-12⁸ 13² (-2, cancelled, with no loss of text). Quires are signed in small roman numerals, verso of last leaf, middle lower margin (some cut away).

Written above the top ruled line in a twelfth-century minuscule; letters tend to be very even and rectangular in shape; straight 's,' 'd' and 'r' predominate; 'ae' often written as e-cedilla.

Twenty 7- to 3-line initials drawn in red outline; decoratively shaped with leafy-vines sprouting from the initials, or zoomorphic; infilled with vines, also in red outline, on blue, yellow or green (used in combination and alone); some initials on unbounded blue grounds which follow the shape of the initial. Two 4- to 5-line red initials, ff. 42 and 43v, with simple pen flourishes in red or red and blue. Chapters begin with 2-line initials, usually red, but occasionally blue or green; some with simple pen flourishes. Red rubrics, running titles and line-fillers (blue used rarely for headings). Opening words following major initials copied in colored capitals, in a display script, or highlighted in red. Majuscules within the text daubed in red. Purchased by Philip Hofer from Erik von Scherling, May, 1954 (*Rotulus* 7 [1954] no. 2479, with plate of f. 77v). Deposited by Hofer in the library, 1 January 1967; accession record: *68M-150(55). Hofer bequest, 1984. Secundo folio (now f. 1): sola nobis.

THE POPULARITY OF GREGORY the Great's *Moralia in Job,* is vividly demonstrated by how often it was imitated, abbreviated, and adapted in other ways by authors throughout the Middle Ages.[1] This laudatory process of imitation and adaptation was even extended second-hand, as it were, to the work of Gregory's notary, Paterius, whose commentary on the Bible was assembled from Gregory's works. Paterius searched through Gregory's works, extracting comments on various biblical passages, and rearranging them in the order of the Bible. Only the first section of this work, the *Liber testimoniorum,* survives, commenting on Genesis through Canticles.[2] A number of twelfth-century authors, in turn, imitated and completed Paterius' text.[3] Our manuscript contains one such twelfth-century commentary by an author known only from his prologue, in which he is identified as Bruno.[4] The evidence of the provenance of the surviving manuscripts suggests that Bruno was most likely a Cistercian monk, and it is possible that the Bernard mentioned in the prologue is the famous Cistercian Abbot, Bernard of Clairvaux (1090-1153).

Bruno corrected Paterius' text, which concludes with Canticles, and then composed his own commentary on the remaining books of the Bible. It is modelled on Paterius, and uses extracts from Gregory's works in the same way. MS Typ 205 is not a complete copy of Bruno's text. It begins in chapter three of the commentary

57

on Acts, and continues with commentaries on the Catholic Epistles, omitting the second Epistle of John and Jude, the Pauline Epistles, with the exception of Philemon, and the Gospels.[5] Bruno's prologue and the commentary on the Apocalypse may have been at the beginning of the manuscript at one time. Bruno's commentary was not copied frequently during the Middle Ages. Stegmüller's *Repertorium biblicum*, the standard reference work for medieval biblical commentaries, lists only twelve copies.[6] With the addition of MS Typ 205, the list can now be expanded to thirteen.

Because of the nature of Bruno's text, this manuscript is organized in an exceptionally sophisticated manner. Chapter lists were copied in a smaller script before the commentary on each book of the Bible; each title in these lists is numbered. The corresponding chapters in the commentary are numbered in the margins, and begin with colored initials that emphasize the divisions of the text. Before each chapter is a heading, copied in red, or in exceptional cases, in blue, which gives a reference to the work of Gregory used in the chapter; the citations to Gregory are quite complete, including the title of the work, the book, and sometimes the chapter. Running titles are also included throughout the manuscript, and indicate which book of the Bible is discussed on the page. This manuscript, unlike the copies of Gregory's *Moralia* (see cat. nos. 19 and 20) also included in this case, is a book that was intended for reference use, and the presentation of the text ensures that readers could find the passages they were looking for efficiently.[7]

BIBLIOGRAPHY: Faye and Bond, 270; *Harvard Cat.* (1955) p. 12, no. 16.

NOTES:

[1] Rene Wasselynck, "Les compilations des 'Moralia in Job' du VII^c au XII^c siècle," *Recherches de théologie ancienne et médiévale* 29 (1962) 5-32.

[2] Wasselynck, "Les compilations," 5-8; Andre Wilmart, "Le Recueil grégorien de Paterius et les fragments Wisigothiques de Paris," *Revue bénédictine* 39 (1927) 81-104; R. Etaix, "Le Liber Testimoniorum de Paterius," *Revue des sciences religieuses* 32 (1958) 66-78; Stegmüller 6264-6277. Printed in *PL* 79:683-916 (Genesis-Canticles); the remaining text in *PL* is not part of Paterius' work, but a compilation by an anonymous twelfth-century author, see note 3, below.

[3] Wasselynck, "Les compilations," 23-25; one such compilation is printed in *PL* 79: 917-1136, where it is incorrectly identified as Paterius, and listed in Stegmüller 6278-6316 as Ps-Paterius A. Another is the *Gregoriale* by Alulfus (d. 1141), a monk at St. Martin's of Tournai; the last part of this work is printed in *PL* 79:1137-1424, and listed in Stegmüller as Ps-Paterius C, 6320-6320,3.

[4] Only the prologue (not included in MS Typ 205) to the work has been printed; see *PL* 79: 681-684; Stegmüller 6317-6319.24. On Bruno's commentary, see Wasselynck, "Les compilations," 25-27; and Wilmart, "Le Recueil grégorien de Paterius," 98.

[5] Stegmüller 6319,2-6319,7; [6319,8 omitted]; 6319,9-6319,24.

[6] Stegmüller, vol. 4, lists 9 manuscripts; 3 additional manuscripts listed in the *Supplement*, vol. 9.

[7] For further discussion of this topic, see cat. no. 23.

22. Gospel Harmony, with the preface by Victor of Capua

Belgium (Meuse valley) or Germany (?) s. XII³/⁴   MS Richardson 25

Parchment (thick and soft), ff. i + 87 + i, 285 x 190 (208 x 111-109) mm. 30 long lines. Ruled lightly in lead; double full-length vertical bounding lines. Prickings in three outer margins.

1-10⁸ 11⁸ (-8, following f. 86, cancelled with no loss of text; + 8, later parchment leaf with notes, s. XIV-XV). Signed in red roman numerals, decoratively boxed, verso of last leaf of each quire, middle, lower margin.

Written in an upright, even, twelfth-century minuscule; 'pp' written separately; 'ae' often written e-cedilla; straight 'd,' and 's' predominate, although round 's' is used finally; minims with finishing strokes turning upwards; round letters formed with a number of broken strokes.

One 5-line red initial with simple shadowing in red, f. 1 (preface); blank space for 10-line 'Q,' with a tail of 6 additional lines, f. 6 (text). 3-line undecorated red initial, f. 2v (beginning of chapter list); 1- to 2-line undecorated red initials throughout, at the beginning of new sections within the text, placed in the inner margin between the double vertical bounding lines. Red rubrics and numbers in the marginal apparatus and chapter lists. Majuscules within the text stroked with red, or highlighted with red dots. Belonged to William King Richardson; Richardson bequest, March 1, 1951. Accession record: *50M-279. Secundo folio: lectionem ante et.

Since the very early days of the Church, scholars have puzzled over the problems posed by the existence of four different accounts of Christ's life and ministry. The Eusebian Canon tables, discussed above (cat. no. 5), were designed to make it easier to compare the accounts in the different Gospels. The text in this manuscript approaches the problem from a different angle, by combining the text of the four Gospels into one continuous narrative. This Gospel Harmony is descended from the text of the Gospels in a famous copy of the New Testament, the Codex Fuldensis, which was written for Victor, bishop of Capua (bishop from 541; d. 554), and later owned by St. Boniface (d. 754). In our manuscript, as well as in other copies, the Gospel Harmony is accompanied by a preface written by Victor. It was once argued that Victor translated a Gospel Harmony based on the second-century *Diatessaron* of Tatian into Latin, and corrected its text to bring it into agreement with the Vulgate. Modern scholars, however, generally agree that the Latin Harmony based on the Vulgate in the Codex Fuldensis was already in existence in Victor of Capua's day. His role was probably the much more modest one of writing the prologue, and adding the indications of the Eusebian Canon Tables at the appropriate places in the text of the Gospel Harmony.[1]

It is likely that manuscripts such as this one were used during the Middle Ages primarily for private study and meditation, in much the same fashion as Gospel Harmonies are used today. Copies of the New Testament like the Codex Fuldensis in which a Gospel Harmony replaces the text of the four independent Gospels never became common, although the text of the Gospels in some copies of the Bible and in some liturgical books was influenced by readings taken from Harmonies of the Gospels. The numerous marginal notes added to our copy of this

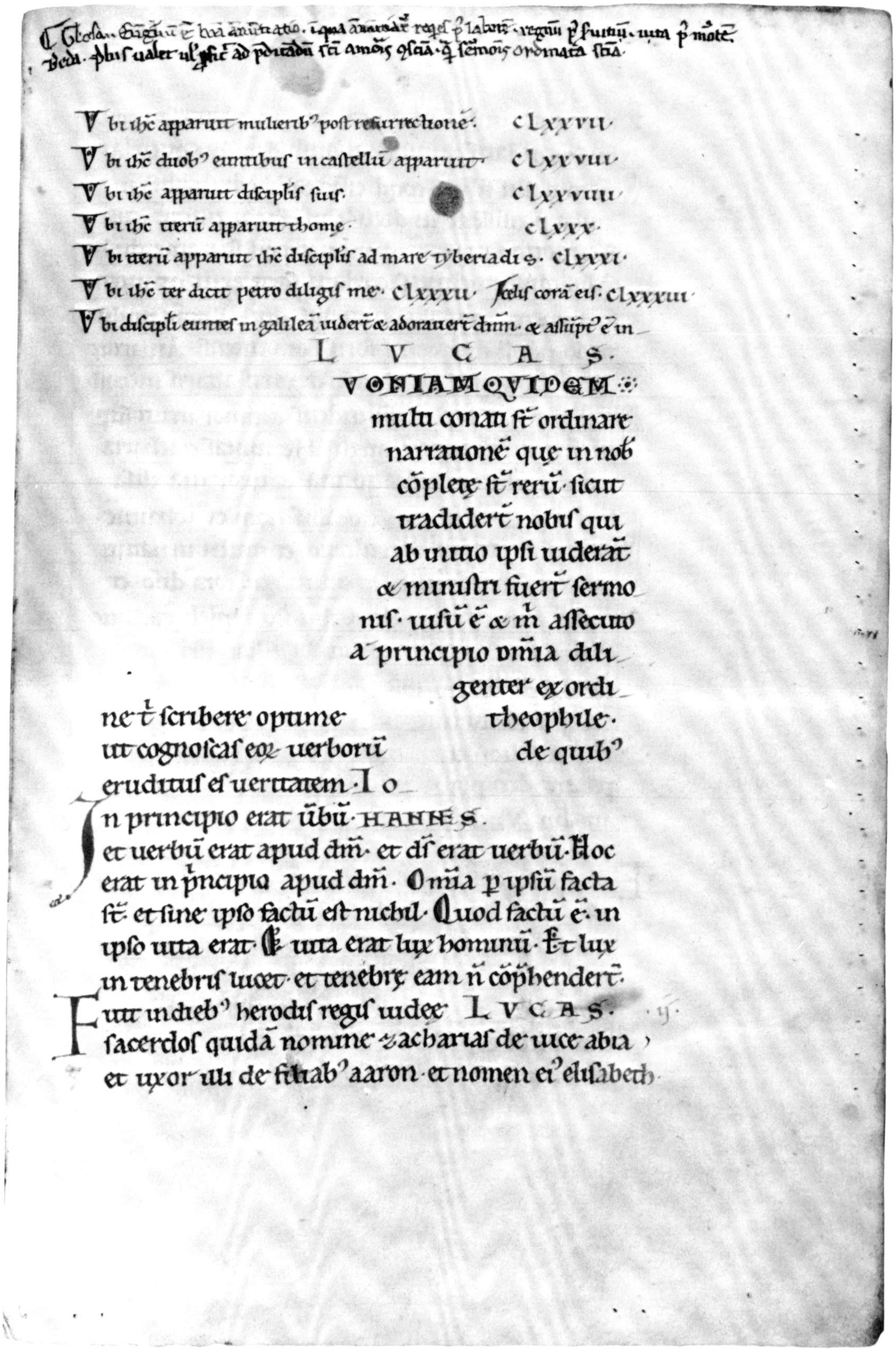

¶ Glosam dicunt ē hoi anutatio. i qua auuisdat reges p̄ labris regnii p̄ sustiū. uita p̄ mortē.
Beda. plus ualet ul'psic ad portadū sm amoris gloria. q̄ seruois ordinata stā.

Vbi ihc apparuit mulierib; post resurrectione·   CLXXVII
Vbi ihc duob; euntibus in castellū apparuit·   CLXXVIII
Vbi ihc apparuit disciplis suis·   CLXXVIIII
Vbi ihc iteru apparuit thome·   CLXXX
Vbi iteru apparuit ihc disciplis ad mare tyberiadi s. CLXXXI
Vbi ihc ter dicit petro diligis me· CLXXXII   Scelus corā eis· CLXXXIII
Vbi discipli euntes in galilea uiderūt & adorauerūt dm̄. & assūpsi ē in

            L V C A S.

        VONIAM QVIDEM ·:·
        multi conati sū ordinare
        narratione que in nob
        cōplete sū rerū sicut
        tradiderūt nobis qui
        ab initio ipsi uiderāt
        & ministri fuerūt sermo
        nis· uisū ē & m̄ assecuto
        a principio ōmia dili
                genter ex ordi
ne t scribere optime   theophile.
ut cognoscas eoꝛ uerborū   de quib;
eruditus es ueritatem I o
In principio erat ūbū· HANNES.
et uerbū erat apud dm̄. et ds̄ erat uerbū· Hoc
erat in pncipio apud dm̄. Omnia p ipsū facta
sū· et sine ipso factū est nichil· Quod factū ē· in
ipso uita erat & uita erat lux hominū· Et lux
in tenebris lucet· et tenebre eam n̄ cōphenderūt·
Fuit in dieb; herodis regis iudee· L V C A S.
sacerdos quidā nomine zacharias de uice abia
et uxor illi de filiab; aaron· et nomen ei' elisabeth

Plate 15. No. 22. MS Richardson 25, f. 6. 4/5 actual size.

60

text, usually taken from patristic and medieval commentaries, indicate that it was used in the thirteenth and fourteenth centuries for study.

The popularity of this Gospel Harmony in the twelfth century is demonstrated by the success of the commentary composed by the Premonstratensian Canon, Zachary of Besançon (also known as Zacharias Chrysopolitanus), soon after 1150-2. Numerous manuscripts of this lengthy work, many of them expensive, carefully written and decorated copies, survive.[2]

BIBLIOGRAPHY: De Ricci, 2300 (= Boston, Library of W. K. Richardson, MS 25); cf. Faye and Bond, 246.

NOTES:

[1]Edited by Ernestus Ranke, *Codex Fuldensis: Novum Testamentum latine interprete Hieronymo ex manuscripto Victoris Capuani* (Marburg and Leipzig 1868) 1-165; also printed in *PL* 68:251-358; *CPL* 953a; Stegmüller 1279; cf. H. J. Vogels, *Beiträge zur Geschichte des Diatessaron im Abendlande.* Neutestamentliche Abhandlungen 8, Hft. 1 (1919), and

Donatien de Bruyne, "La préface de Diatessaron latin avant Victor de Capoue," *Revue bénédictine* 39 (1927) 6-11.

[2]Stegmüller 8400, listing over 50 manuscripts; printed in *PL* 186:11-620; cf. D. Van de Eynde, "Les Magistri du Commentaire 'Unum ex quatuor' de Zacharias Chrysopolitanus," *Antonianum* 23 (1948) 1-32; 181-220.

23.   Augustine, Commentary on the First Epistle of John

Germany (Weissenau?) s. XII[1]   MS Lat 213 (formerly MS Norton 2000)

Parchment (stiff and smooth), ff. ii + 92 + ii, 236 x 161 (177-174 x 122-116) mm. 25 long lines. Ruled in hard point with the top 2 and bottom 2 or 3 horizontal lines full across; single full-length vertical bounding lines. Prickings, top, bottom and occasionally outer margins.

1-11⁸ 12⁴.

Written above the top ruled line in a twelfth-century minuscule; script is very regular, with markedly rectangular letter forms and flat horizontal finishing strokes on minims, ascenders and descenders; 'ae' usually written e-cedilla, straight 'r,' 'd' and 's' predominate, although round 's' is used finally, and round 'd' occasionally occurs.

One 8-line initial, f. 1, outlined in red-orange, infilled with a white-vine on pale yellow, fancifully intertwined and terminating in large pointed leaves, with highlights in orange-red and green wash, and with a grotesque (winged wolf or dog) sitting within the vine. Homilies begin with 4- to 2-line red initials. Red rubrics; on f. 1, within the text space and brushed with pale yellow wash; remaining rubrics copied in the margin. Passages summarizing the scriptural text at the beginning of each homily daubed with red, or with a red line drawn through the letters. Opening words of the text in fanciful capitals or semi-rustics, ff. 1 (daubed with red), 30, 63, 73, and 82v. Belonged to Charles Eliot Norton; purchased, March 14, 1906, with funds from the friends of the library. Secundo folio: res quae solo corde.

AUGUSTINE'S *Commentary on the First Epistle of John*, originated as a series of homilies, which were likely preached in 416.[1] Augustine specifies in the prologue that he is interrupting his series of homilies on the Gospel of John in order to remain in harmony with the cycle of liturgical readings. He chose to comment on John's Epistle because it was a text which he felt was suitable for the Easter season. This prologue and other passages in the commentary have provided scholars with valuable clues towards reconstructing the cycle of liturgical readings current in Augustine's lifetime.[2] The Epistle with its emphasis on charity, moreover, was particularly well suited to Augustine's own inclinations. Throughout his works he emphasizes that the purpose of studying Scripture is to increase the love of God and of our neighbors:

> But when I was thinking what matter of discourse upon the Scriptures, agreeably with the cheerfulness of these days, I might undertake with you . . .; the Epistle of blessed John occurred to me: that whereas we have for a while intermitted the reading of his Gospel, we may in discoursing upon his Epistle not go from his side: the rather, as in this same Epistle, which is very sweet to all who have a healthy taste of the heart to relish the Bread of God, and very meet to be had in remembrance in God's Holy Church, charity is above all commended.[3]

This copy of Augustine's Commentary belonged to the Premonstratensian Canons at Weissenau in Bavaria in the eighteenth century, and it is quite possible that it was written there.[4] The simple organization used in this manuscript, which dates from the first half of the twelfth century, may usefully be compared with the two later manuscripts included in this case. Each homily begins with an initial, and every homily except the first is prefaced by a summary of the scriptural text discussed in that homily. The homilies are unnumbered, and lack rubrics and internal divisions.

MS Richardson 14 (see cat. no. 24) was copied in the second half of the century. Its original layout was similar to that used in MS Lat 213. Soon after it was made, however, a second writer added a number of features which make it a much easier book to use for reference. This writer added a chapter list on f. 1v, a single leaf added to the beginning of the first quire. He also added numbers corresponding to these chapters in the margins of the text, and either drew a red line through the opening words of each chapter, or recopied them in red.

The layout in fMS Typ 200 (see cat. no. 25), which dates from the early thirteenth century, is even more sophisticated, and incorporates a number of features which were to become standard over the course of the thirteenth century. It is divided into twenty books, numbered in the rubrics, and an additional unnumbered section. Chapter lists and clearly delineated, numbered chapters, are also used, although in this manuscript they are used only for the first ten books. The chapters in the remaining books are unnumbered.[5] Biblical citations within the text are indicated in the margin by the customary marks. The names of other authors cited in the text are also identified in the margins. Two later hands added indications of the biblical chapter discussed in the commentary in the running titles and in the margins.

In thirteenth-century manuscripts, devices which we generally take for granted, such as numbered chapters, chapter lists or tables of contents, marginal identification of the citations, and running headlines, are quite common. These aids to the reader make it much quicker to find passages within the text, and their use reflects the fact that many manuscripts were intended to be used for study and for reference. In the second half of the twelfth-century, the consistent use of such aids is fairly rare, and a careful study of the organization and layout of manuscripts from this period is therefore of special interest.[6]

BIBLIOGRAPHY: De Ricci, 998 (= MS Norton 2000); Faye and Bond, 241; Arthur Stanley Pease, "A Harvard Manuscript of St. Augustine," *Harvard Studies in Classical Philology* 21 (1910) 51-74.

NOTES:

[1]Augustine, *In epistolam Ioannis ad Parthos tractatus X*; printed in *PL* 35:1977-2062, and, with French translation, in P. Agaësse, *Commentaire de la première Epître de S. Jean.* Sources Chrétiennes 75 (Paris 1984); *CPL* 279; Stegmüller 1477.

[2]See S. Poque, "Les lectures liturgiques de l'octave pascale à Hippone d'après les traités de S. Augustin sur la première épître de S. Jean," *Revue bénédictine* 74 (1964) 217-241.

[3]"Homilies on the First Epistle of John," translated by H. Browne and edited by Joseph H. Myers, in *St Augustin [sic]; Homilies on the Gospel of John; Homilies on the First Epistle of John; Soliloquies.* A Select Library of the Nicene and Post-Nicene Fathers of the Christian Church, Philip Schaff, ed. vol. 7 (Grand Rapids, Michigan 1956) 453-529, this passage, 459-460.

[4]Ex-libris note in ink, top margin, f. 1: "Biblioth. Weissenau."

[5]Except books 14 and 16, beginning ff. 128 and 152, respectively, which are undivided; books 15 and 17, beginning ff. 138v and 160v, have very few chapter divisions; chapters in the commentary on Lamentations, books 18-20 (beginning ff. 170v, 185 and 198) are labelled with the traditional names of the letters in the Hebrew alphabet.

[6]The development of these aids to the reader has been examined in R. H. and M. A. Rouse, "*Statim invenire*: Schools, Preachers and New Attitudes to the Page," in *Renaissance and Renewal in the Twelfth Century*, R. L. Benson and G. Constable, with C. Lanham, eds. (Cambridge, Mass. 1982) 205-209.

24.   Augustine, Contra Faustum Manichaeum

Northern France (Pontigny?) s. XII²   MS Richardson 14

Parchment (creamy, slightly stiff and rough), ff. i + 166 + i, 365 x 255 mm. Layout varies, ff. 1-17v, and 26-end, (255-250 x 175-168) mm. 2 columns, 36 lines; ff. 18-25v, quire 3, (265-263 x 180-178) mm. 2 columns, 39 lines. Ruled in lead, with the top 3 and bottom 2 or 3 horizontal rules full across on most folios (some with top, 3rd from top, penultimate and bottom horizontal rules full across); remaining horizontal rules do not extend across the space between the columns; single full-length vertical bounding lines. Prickings top, bottom and outside margins; quire 10, ff. 74-81v, also with full rows of closely-spaced prickings across the top and bottom margins; quire 17, ff. 130-137v, with 2 rows of prickings, outer margin.

1⁸ (+ 1, f. 1, singleton) 2-18⁸ 19⁸ (1, f. 146, and 8, f. 153, single) 20⁸ 21⁶ (-6, following f. 166, cancelled with no loss of text). Quires signed in roman numerals, usually flourished on all sides, bottom margin, verso of last leaf, just under the right hand column; horizontal catchword, erased but still legible, bottom margin under column b, quire 20, f. 161v.

Written in an upright twelfth-century minuscule, approaching gothic; round 'd' and 'r' used after round letters; some use of e-cedilla for 'ae'; lacks letter unions except for 'pp.'

Two 6- to 5-line red initials (with extensions into the margins up to 20-lines), ff. 1 and 104v, with decorative void spaces within the initials, and simple red pen flourishes. Sections within the text are indicated by red marginal roman numerals, with 1-line red initials or a red line drawn through the opening words, all added soon after the manuscript was completed. Belonged to William King Richardson; Richardson bequest, March 1, 1951. Accession record: *50M-269. Secundo folio (f. 1v capitula list, added in a different hand, soon after the manuscript was completed): [rubric] *Incipit prefatio*, [text] Faustus quidam; [f. 3] uolueris omissis.

BIBLIOGRAPHY: De Ricci, 959 (= Boston, Library of W. K. Richardson, MS 14); cf. Faye and Bond, 246.

25.   Rabanus Maurus, Commentary on Jeremiah and Lamentations

Northern France (Pontigny) s. XIII¹ᐟ⁴   fMS Typ 200

Parchment (fairly thin and rough, both sides), ff. ii + 208 (foliated in pencil, upper, outside margin, cited; paginated in an earlier hand, lower margin, recto only) + ii, 393 x 280 (268 x 184-180) mm. 2 columns, 40 lines. Ruled in lead with the top 3 and bottom 3 horizontal rules full across; single full-length vertical bounding lines with extra single vertical bounding lines in the inner and outer margins. Prickings in all 4 margins.

1-26⁸. Quires signed with roman numerals, middle, bottom margin, verso of last leaf of quire (some partly cut away); horizontal catchwords, bottom, inside margin (many excised).

Written on the top line in an early gothic bookhand; descenders in the last line of text on a page sometimes elongated and decorated with leaf-like terminals in brown ink by the scribe.

Books begin with 8- to 6-line beige or royal blue initials, terminating in leaves or dragons' heads, on deep blue or red grounds; infilled with rinceaux, and foliage, some inhabited by small dogs, birds or dragons, in shades of blue, brown, olive green and yellow. Chapters begin with 2-line alternately bright blue and dull orange-red initials with pen scrolls in the other colors. Red rubrics. Running titles added in a later hand. Belonged to Chester Beatty; his sale, London, Sotheby's, May 9, 1933, vol. 2, no. 44, plate 13 (reproducing f. 2v). Belonged to Philip Hofer; his gift to the library, August 1, 1983, in honor of Roger E. Stoddard. Accession record: *83M-5. Secundo folio: [minu]tus temerario.

INCIPIT PREFATIO AURELII AUGUSTI
DI IN LIBROS CONTRA FAUSTU OQ;
FAUSTUS QUIDA
fuit gente affer. ciuitate
mileuitanus. eloquio fua
uis. ingenio callidus. fecta
manicheus. ac p hoc ne
fando errore puerfus.

Noueram ipfe hominem quem
admodum eum commemoraui in
libris confeffionum meuru. Hic qd
dam uolumen edidit aduerfus rec
tam. xpianam fidem. et catholicam
ueritatem. Quod cum uenisfet
un manus nras lectumq; eet afia
tribus defiderauerunt. et ure ca
ritatis p quã eis feruimus flagtauert.
ut ei responderem. Hoc aggrediar nc
un nomine atq; adiutorio dni et falua
toris nri ihu xpi. ut omf qui hec le
gent intelligant. quam nichil firacu
tum ingenii et lingua expolita nifi
adno greffus hominis dirigantur;
quod multis etiam tardioribz et inua
lidioribus occulta equitate diuine
mifedie preftitum e. cum multi acer
rimi et facundiffimi deferta abadiuto
rio di. ad hoc uelociter et pinacitr
currerent. ut aueritatis uia longius
aberrarent. Comodum aut arbitror
fub eius nomine uerba eius ponere:
et fub meo responsione mea. Fauft
dixit. Satis fupq; in lucem iam tra
ductis erroribus ac iudaice fupfticionis
fimul et femi xpianorú abunde detec
ta fallacia adoctiffimo fcilicet et folo

nobis poft beatu patrem nrm mani che
um ftudendo adimanto ñ ab re tũ
uifum e. fratres lmu hec quoq; bre
uia uobis et concinna responfa propt
callidas et aftutas conferentium nobis
cum propofitiones fcribere. Quo cũ
idem uos ex more parentis fui ferpen
tis captiofis circumuenire queftiun
culis uoluerint. et ipfi ad responden
dum uigilanter eis fitis inftructi.
Ita eñ fiet ut ad ea ipfa que propo
fuerunt religati. ulterius huc atq; il
luc uagari non poffint; ac ne profufa
confufa ue oratione legentium inuin
darentur ingenia. tam breuit quam
diftincte ex aduerfo fibi ipforu atq;
nroru dicta eftenu. Auguftni refpondt.
Tu femi xpianos cauendos putas: quod
nos ee dicis. Nos aut pfeudo xpia
nos cauemus: quod uos ee oftendim.
Nam quod femum e. ex qua dam
parte impfectum. ex nulla tamen fal
fum e. Quid ergo fi aliquid de eft fi
dei eoru quos circumuenire conami
ni. Numquid ideo id quod eis ade
deftruendum: ac non potius id quod
deeft aftruendum e. Sicut & ad qf
dam impfectos loquens apls ait.
Gaudens et uidens uram conuerfa
cionem: et id quod deeft fidei ure
in xpo. Cernebat utiq; quandam
fabricam fpitalem. ficut alibi dicit
di edificatio eftis: et inea cernebat
utru q; et unde gauderet. et un
de faragerret. Gaudebat ex eo quod
iam edificatum uidebat: faragebat

adimatus ut
adimandus ufr
fuit qdã doctr
manicheoi.

I
INCIPIT LIBER PRIOR

Plate 16. No. 24. MS Richardson 14, f. 2. 3/5 actual size.

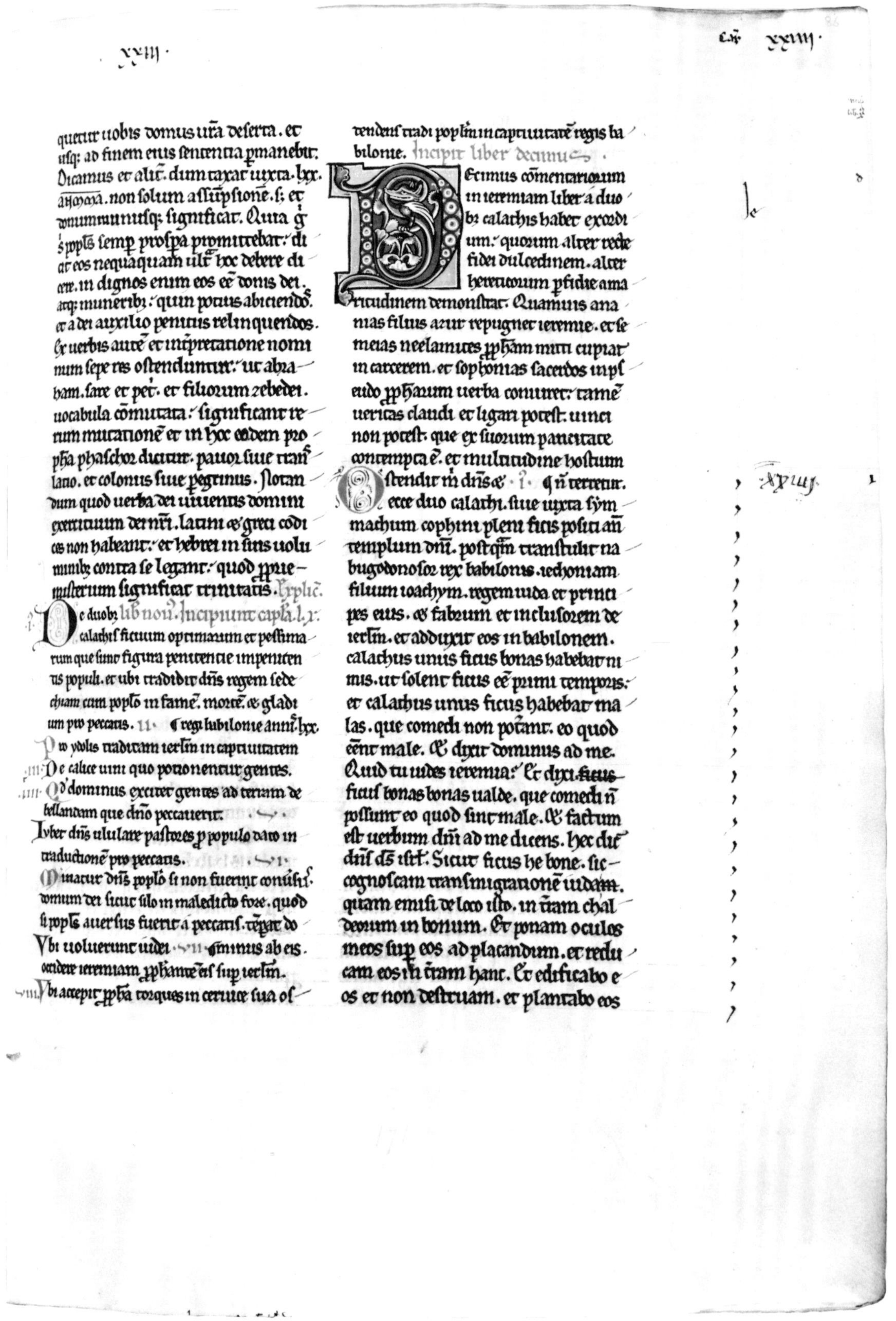

Plate 17. No. 25. fMS Typ 200, f. 86. 1/2 actual size.

BIBLIOGRAPHY: De Ricci, 1696 (= New York, Collection of Philip Hofer, MS 20); Faye and Bond, 270; E. G. Millar, *The Library of A. Chester Beatty; a Descriptive Catalogue of the Western Manuscripts* (Oxford 1927) 1:117-18, no. 35, plate LXXXVI (reproducing f. 11v); *Harvard Cat* (1955) p. 13, no. 20 and plate 20 (reproducing f. 1v); Dorothy Miner, "Since De Ricci — Western Illuminated Manuscripts Acquired Since 1934; Part 2," *The Journal of the Walters Art Gallery* 31-32 (1968-69) 60; Walter Cahn, "A Twelfth-Century Decretum Fragment from Pontigny," *The Bulletin of the Cleveland Museum of Art* 62 (1975) 53 n. 22; de Hamel, *Glossed Books*, p. 46, n. 43.

THE CISTERCIAN ABBEY OF ST. MARY at Pontigny near Auxerre in Burgundy, was an early daughter house of Cîteaux, established in 1114 by St. Bernard. The foundation flourished, and by the second half of the twelfth century it was famous for its library.[1] A list of the Pontigny's books, compiled in the late twelfth or early thirteenth century survives in a copy of Ralph of Flaix, Commentary on Leviticus, now Montpellier, Bibliothèque de l'Ecole de Médecine, MS 12.[2] It is an impressively long list, including almost 200 volumes. The size of this collection may be compared with the much more modest library at Morimondo, which possessed about sixty volumes when the late twelfth-century book list in fMS Typ 223 was compiled (see cat. nos. 1 and 10). The volume of Augustine's *Contra Faustum* listed in the catalogue may possibly be our copy of this text, MS Richardson 14.[3] Rabanus' Commentary on Jeremiah, the text included in fMS Typ 200,[4] is not listed in this catalogue, although it appears in catalogues of the library made at later dates.[5]

Early in the nineteenth century a group of manuscripts from Pontigny were in the possession of Abbé Joseph Felix Allard of Paris (1795-1831), who sold them to Sir Thomas Phillipps, sometime between 1824 and 1828. Included in this group of manuscripts were both MS Richardson 14 and fMS Typ 200.[6] The traditional attribution of MS Richardson 14 to Pontigny is based largely on the fact that it was among the books sold by Allard to Phillipps. The evidence that fMS Typ 200 once belonged to the monastery is stronger, since it is very similar to a number of other manuscripts which include thirteenth-century ex-libris notes from Pontigny.[7]

A comparison of these two manuscripts raises an interesting question related to the production of books in Cistercian Monasteries. Early Cistercian statutes decreed that books should be decorated in only the most sober fashion: "Letters should be made of one color and without illustration [*non depictae*]."[8] The decoration in MS Richardson 14, which dates from the second half of the twelfth century, is confined to two large red initials at the beginning of the major divisions within the text. It is a book which easily conforms to the letter of the statute. fMS Typ 200, dating from the early years of the thirteenth century, however, includes painted initials at the beginning of each book of the commentary. These large initials are decorated with scrolls and foliage within the initials; some include small dogs, birds and dragons lurking within the scrolls.[9] This volume, therefore, does not conform with the Cistercian legislation.

The importance of this contradiction between precept and practice, however, can easily be exaggerated. Recent scholarship has demonstrated that Cistercian monasteries acquired illuminated manuscripts through gifts and commissions.[10] The range of decoration in books made at Cistercian monasteries, moreover, is much broader than once was supposed. MS Richardson 14 is an example of a book with very restrained decoration. The famous Bible from Clairvaux, Troyes, Bibliothèque Municipale, MS 27, with its very handsome painted initials in one color, is an example of a manuscript decorated in a style which followed the letter, if not the spirit, of the legislation.[11] More elaborate books, with painted initials in different colors, some with grotesques like fMS Typ 200, were also produced.[12] Finally, manuscripts such as the Heisterbach Bible, Berlin, Staatsbibliothek, MS theol. lat. 379, and the Pontigny Bible fragments, Paris, Bibliothèque Nationale, MS lat. 8823, are examples of lavish manuscripts, decorated with gold and figurative initials, which were certainly owned by Cistercian monasteries, and may well have been made by the Cistercians.[13] The argument that any particular manuscript is too lavish to be Cistercian in provenance is therefore questionable. The two manuscripts shown here exemplify only two of the various trends in Cistercian manuscript decoration.

FURTHER READING: for a balanced summary on the problem of Cistercian illumination, with numerous references to earlier works, see Walter Cahn, "The *Rule* and the Book: Cistercian Book Illumination in Burgundy and Champagne," *Monasticism and the Arts*, Timothy Gregory Verdon and John Dally, eds. (Syracuse 1984) 139-172.

NOTES:

[1]C. H. Talbot, "Notes on the Library of Pontigny," *Analecta sacri ordinis cisterciensis* 10 (1954) 106-108; de Hamel, *Glossed Books*, 44-45; Dorothy Miner, "Since De Ricci — Western Illuminated Manuscripts Acquired Since 1934; Part 2," *Journal of the Walters Art Gallery* 31-32 (1968-9) 57.

[2]Printed in *Catalogue général des manuscrits de bibliothèques publiques de Départements* Quarto series, 1 (Paris 1849), appendix, 697-717.

[3]*Catalogue général*, quarto series 1, 697: "Volumen unum contra Faustum hereticum, libris duodecim"; since the books are simply listed by title, there is no proof that this is our copy; Augustine, *Contra Faustum manichaeum,* Joseph Zycha, ed. in Corpus scriptorum ecclesiasticorum latinorum 25, sect. 6, part 1 (1891) 251-797; *CPL* 321.

[4]Ed. in *PL* 111:793-1272; Stegmüller 7504-7505.

[5]C. H. Talbot, in "Notes on the Library of Pontigny," published four later inventories of the library. The catalogue compiled by Charles De Tonnellier in 1675 lists Augustine, *Contra Faustum* (p. 112), and Rabanus Maurus, On Jeremiah (p. 113); in the 1734 inventory compiled by M.

L'Abbé Le Boeuf, Augustine is not listed, but the Rabanus Commentary is (p. 120); the last abbot of Pontigny, Jean Depaquy, compiled a careful inventory in 1778: no. 127, "Augustinus contra Faustum in 4° (see page 132)"; and no. 172, "Rabanus Maurus, in Jeremiam prophetarum, in 4° max. (see p. 135)"; the list compiled in 1794 by the commissioners also lists both these works: no. 209, "Augustinus, contra Faustum et de vita patriarchum, MS. velin XII s. in fol. integer et eleg. (see p. 144)"; it may be noted that if this entry can be identified with MS Richardson 14, it is evidence that it once included a second text; and no. 222, "Rabanus Maurus, Expositionis in Jeremiam lib. XX, cod. memb. XIII s., in fol. eleg. et integ. (see p. 149)." Talbot identified the Rabanus Maurus, no. 172 in Depaquy's catalogue, as fMS Typ 200 (listed as Chester Beatty MS 35, olim Phillipps MS 3726) p. 162; he does not list MS Richardson 14.

[6]MS Richardson 14, formerly Phillipps MS 3720; fMS Typ 200, formerly Phillipps MS 3726; see A. N. L. Munby, *The Phillipps Manuscripts: Catalogus librorum manu-*

scriptorum in bibliotheca D. Thomae Phillipps, BT. Impressum typis Medio-Montanis, 1837-1871, reprint, (London 1968) 47; A. N. L. Munby, *The Formation of the Phillipps Library up to the Year 1840*, Phillipps Studies 3 (Cambridge 1954) 33, and appendix (MSS 3714-3754, Ex bibliotheca M. Allard, with a note that "the ecclesiastical writers in this collection seem to have belonged to Pontigny abbey."); and Talbot, "Notes on the library of Pontigny," 157-8.

[7]Rabanus Maurus, Commentary on Numbers, present location unknown, formerly Phillipps 3274 and no. 90 in Quaritch's *Catalogue of Illuminated Manuscripts* (1931); Rabanus Maurus, Commentary on Deuteronomy, London, British Library Additional MS 38687 (formerly Phillipps 3725), which includes a contemporary ex-libris from Pontigny (see Millar, *The Library of A. Chester Beatty*, 117-118); and Rabanus Maurus, Commentary on Matthew, London, University College, MS Lat 7 (formerly Phillipps 3727). fMS Typ 200 is also related to Baltimore, Walters Art Gallery, MS W. 778, Haymo, Commentary on the Pauline Epistles (formerly Phillipps 3737, obtained from Allard; and formerly Chester Beatty MS 36), which includes an early ex-libris note from Pontigny (see Dorothy Miner, "Since De Ricci," 57-60, and figures 11-13). These four manuscripts are listed in Talbot, "Notes on the library of Pontigny," 162-3, nos. 162, 166, 167 and 173.

[8]Cited from Walter Cahn, "The *Rule* and the Book: Cistercian Book Illumination in Burgundy and Champagne,"

Monasticism and the Arts, Timothy Gregory Verdon and John Dally, eds. (Syracuse 1984) 140-1 and notes 8 and 9; art. 82 of the *Instituta*; a number of different dates for this article have been suggested, including 1134 and 1151.

[9]They are a late example of Channel style decoration, similar to the initial cut from a Bible, possibly also from Pontigny, fMS Typ 315 (cat. no. 2), discussed earlier; on this style, see C. R. Dodwell, *The Canterbury School of Illumination: 1066-1200* (Cambridge 1954) 104-109; Walter Cahn, "St. Albans and the Channel Style in England," *The Year 1200; A Symposium* (New York 1975) 187-229; and Rodney M. Thomson, *Manuscripts from St. Albans Abbey, 1066-1235* (Woodbridge, Suffolk 1982) 1:51-62, especially 54-55; cf. de Hamel, *Glossed Books*, 45-54 and 80-82.

[10]See especially Walter Cahn, "The *Rule* and the Book," 139-172, a balanced survey of the question.

[11]Cahn, "The *Rule* and the Book," 155 and fig. 6.13.

[12]Cf. for example Yale University, Beinecke Library, MS 349, discussed in Cahn, "The *Rule* and the Book," 143, and fig. 6.1.

[13]Cahn, "The *Rule* and the Book," discussing Berlin, Staatsbibliothek, MS theol. lat. fol. 379 on p. 143 and fig. 16.2; and Paris, BN MS lat. 8823 on p. 164; Cahn suggests that the Pontigny Bible may have been made outside of the monastery. The Pontigny Bible fragments are also discussed above, cat. no. 2.

26. Bede, Commentary on Luke
Germany (Gladbach?) s. XII²/⁴   fMS Typ 202

Parchment, ff. i (paper) + ii (parchment leaves from another manuscript) + 182 + i (parchment leaf from another manuscript), 297 x 206 (231-225 x 151-149) mm. 34 long lines. Ruled in hard point with the top 2 and bottom 2 horizontal rules full across; single full-length vertical bounding lines. Prickings in the three outer margins.

1-15⁸ 16⁸ (-2, following f. 121, and -6, following f. 124, cancelled with no loss of text) 17-23⁸. Quires are signed in roman numerals, middle, lower margin, verso of last leaf.

Written in an even, well-spaced twelfth-century minuscule; chapter list, ff. 4-5v, and biblical lemmata copied in a smaller script with elongated ascenders and descenders (decorated in the last line on a page).

One large unframed drawing in brown pen of Bede presenting his book to Bishop Acca, f. 1. Seven 15- to 7 line initials, drawn in outline in brown or red, with internal scrolls, foliage and dragons' heads; some with dragons forming part of the body of the initial. Two 4- to 3-line undecorated red initials, used at the beginning of Bede's prefatory letter and the chapter list. Biblical lemmata begin with 1-line red initials; commentary following these passages begins with 1-line initials, black ink, usually infilled with red dots. Red rubrics in display script; opening words following large initials copied in larger red capitals. Fifteenth-century ex-libris note from the Benedictine monastery of St. Vitus at Gladbach near Cologne. Belonged to Chester Beatty; his sale, London, Sotheby's, June 7, 1932, vol. I, no. 7 and plate 8 (reproducing f. 1v). Belonged to Philip Hofer; his gift to the library, 1 August 1983, in honor of James E. Walsh. Accession number: *83M-3. Secundo folio: de questionibus.

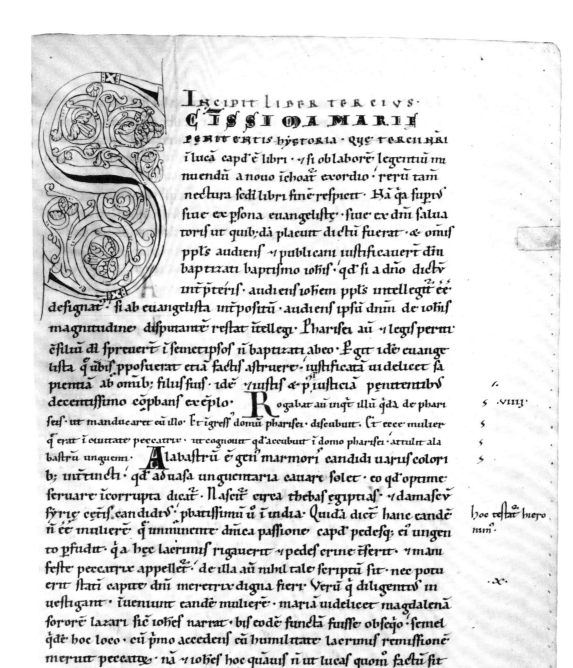

INCIPIT LIBER TERCIVS·

CISSIO MARIE

PENITENTIS HYSTORIA· QVE TERCII HRI
i luca capd̃ ē libri· ⁊ si oblabore legentiũ m
nuendũ a nouo īchoat exordio· rerũ tam
nectura sedi libri fine respicit· Hā q̃a supiꝰ
siue ex p̃sona euangeliste· siue ex dn̄i salua
toris ut quib;dã placuit dictũ fuerat· ⁊ oīs
ppl̃s audiens ⁊ publicani iustificauer̃t dn̄m
baptizati baptismo iohis·qd̃ si a dn̄o dictũ
īt p̃teris· audiens iohem ppl̃s intellegit ee
designat· si ab euangelista īt positũ· audiens ipsũ dn̄m de iohis
magnitudine disputante restat itellegi· Pharisei aũ ⁊ legis periti
c̃siliũ dī spreuer̃t i semetipsos ñ baptizati abeo· Egit ideo euange
lista q̃ ubis ꝓposuerat etia factis astruere· iustificatã uidelicet sa
pientiã ab omib; filiis suis· idē ⁊iustis ⁊ p̃ iusticia penitentibꝰ
decentissimo cõp̃bans exeplo· Rogabat aũ inq̃t illũ q̃da de phari
seis· ut manducaret cũ illo· Et igress̃ domũ pharisei discubuit· Et ecce mulier
q̃ erat i ciuitate peccatrix· ut cognouit qd̃ accubuit i domo pharisei· attulit ala
bastrũ unguenti· Alabastrũ ē gen̄ marmori candidi uariis colori
b; uttincti· qd̃ ad uasa unguentaria cauare solet· eo qd̃ optime
seruare icorrupta dicat· Nascit̃ circa thebas egiptias· ⁊ damascũ
syrie ceteris· candidiꝰ· p̃batissimũ ũ i india· Quidã dicũt hanc cande
ñ ee mulierẽ· q̃ imminente dn̄ica passione· capd̃ pedesq; ei ungen
to p̃fudit· q̃a hec lacrimis rigauerit ⁊ pedes crine iserit· ⁊ mani
feste peccatrix appellet̃· de illa aũ nihil tale scriptũ sit· nec potu
erit stati capite dn̄i meretrix digna fieri· Verũ q̃ diligentiꝰ in
uestigant· iueniunt eandẽ mulierẽ· maria uidelicet magdalenã
sororẽ lazari· sic iohes narrat· bis eode functa fuisse obsecio· semel
q̃dẽ hoc loco· cũ p̃mo accedens cũ humilitate lacrimis remissionẽ
meruit peccatox· nā ⁊iohes hoc q̃uis ñ ut lucas quom̃ factũ sit
narrauerit· tam ipsã mariã cõmdans cõmemorauit ubi de re
suscitando fr̃e ei c̃epit loq̃· erat aũ q̃dã iquiens languens lazarꝰ
a bethania de castello marie ⁊ marthe sororis ei· maria aũ erat

s· viiij
s
s
s

hoc restat inero
nuñ·

·x·

Plate 18. No. 26. fMS Typ 202, f. 68. 7/10 actual size.

70

THE BIBLICAL COMMENTARIES of the Venerable Bede (673-735) can usefully be seen as transitional works. Bede is often considered the last of the Fathers. In some senses, his works can also be seen as the beginning of the medieval commentary tradition. Biblical commentaries form a major part of Bede's writings. The manuscript exhibited here is a copy of his Commentary on the Gospel of Luke.[1] He also composed commentaries on the opening chapters of Genesis, and on the books of Kings, Ezra and Nehemiah, Tobit, Proverbs, the Song of Songs, the Gospel of Mark, Acts, and the Pauline and Catholic Epistles. Bede's own appraisal of these commentaries is found in the summary of his works which he appended to his *Ecclesiastical History*:

> From the time I became a priest until [this] the fifty-ninth year of my life, I have made it my business, for my own benefit and that of my brothers, to make brief extracts from the works of the venerable Fathers on Holy Scripture, or to add notes of my own to clarify their sense and interpretation.[2]

The importance of Bede's "notes of his own" on the Bible should not be underestimated. In his later commentaries especially, more of his work is original than was once stressed.[3] Of particular interest here, however, is the fact that extracts from biblical commentaries by patristic authors do form an important part of many of Bede's commentaries. This characteristic was once cited as a criticism of Bede's work.[4] Such an appraisal misses the important contribution that Bede's transmission of the texts of earlier commentators represents. In selecting, arranging, and commenting on these texts, he presented them in a fashion which was applicable to the new conditions of the Middle Ages, and ensured their survival.

This process of preserving and reinterpreting the patristic heritage continued after Bede's death. Rabanus Maurus (d. 856), the author of the commentary on Jeremiah in fMS Typ 200 (see cat. no. 25), also composed commentaries on many books of the Bible; his reliance on other authors is even more pronounced than was Bede's. Without his work, and the work of other ninth- and tenth-century scholars, the more original commentaries of the eleventh, and especially the twelfth centuries, would have been impossible. The Ordinary Gloss on the Bible, which we will examine in the next section of the exhibition (cat. nos. 30-37), was in many ways a new departure, but it was also an endeavor firmly grounded in the traditional process of collecting, arranging, and finally evaluating, the patristic commentaries.

Preserved in this copy of Bede's Commentary are three leaves from an eleventh-century Bible, which were used as extra leaves before the beginning and end of the text when the book was bound in the fifteenth century. These leaves, which have survived in such a fortuitous manner, are important witnesses to the Old Latin text of the book of Judith.[5]

BIBLIOGRAPHY: De Ricci, 1696 (= New York, Collection of Philip Hofer, MS 19); Faye and Bond, 270; E. G. Millar, *The Library of A. Chester Beatty; a Descriptive Catalogue of Western Manuscripts* (Oxford 1927) 1:107-109, no. 31, appendix II, and plate LXXXII (reproducing f. 1v); *Harvard Cat.* (1955) p. 11, no. 11, cover (reproducing f. 1) and plate 4 (reproducing f. 1 and 1v). FURTHER READING: an excellent introduction to Bede may be found in the essays collected in *Famulus Christi; Essays in Commemoration of the Thirteenth Centenary of the Birth of the Venerable Bede*, Gerald Bonner, ed. (London 1976).

NOTES:

[1] D. Hurst, O.S.B., ed. in CC 120 (Turnholt 1960) 1-425, listing this manuscript, p. vi (as Chester Beatty MS 31); Stegmüller 1614 (listing this manuscript as Cheltenham, Phillipps MS 1092); *CPL* 1356.

[2] *Bede's Ecclesiastical History*, ed. B. Colgrave and R. A. B. Mynors (Oxford 1969) 567, cited in Paul Meyvaert, "Bede the Scholar," *Famulus Christi; Essays in Commemoration of the Thirteenth Centenary of the Birth of the Venerable Bede*, Gerald Bonner, ed. (London 1976) 44.

[3] Meyvaert, "Bede the Scholar," 40-69.

[4] Meyvaert, "Bede the Scholar," 41-45, and 62, discussing and refuting the traditional negative appraisals of this aspect of Bede's work.

[5] Printed in E. G. Millar, *The Library of A. Chester Beatty; a Descriptive Catalogue of Western Manuscripts* (Oxford 1927) vol. 1, appendix II; the Old Latin text of Judith has been studied by M. Bogaert; on this manuscript see, "Un témoin liturgique de la vieille version latine du livre de Judith," *Revue bénédictine* 77 (1967) 14, note 1, and "La version latine du livre de Judith dans la première bible d'Alcala," *Revue bénédictine* 78 (1968) 13, 191-2.

27. Jerome, Commentary on Daniel
Central Italy or Tuscany s. XII[2/4]   fMS Lat 168

Parchment (white and thin), ff. 32, 320 x 220 (233-230 x 135-129) mm. 36 long lines. Ruled in hard point, with the top 2, middle 2, and bottom 2 horizontal rules full across, and with the remaining rules extending past the inner bounding line into the margin; single full-length vertical bounding lines, with an additional bounding line near the gutter on some folios. Neat slash-type prickings, outer margin, and on some folios, in the top and bottom margins.

1-4[8]. Horizontal catchwords, bottom, inside margin.

Written in a clear, rounded, "reformed" twelfth-century minuscule. Display scripts used for the rubrics and the first line of each new section (uncial used, ff. 1 and 12).

Blank spaces remain for 6- to 5-line initials (ff. 1, 2 and 12); crude initials, black ink, supplied by a later hand, ff. 1 and 2. 2-line plain red initials, ff. 30v and 32. Purchased, March 18, 1941 from H. P. Kraus (Treat fund). Secundo folio: magnitudo lectori.

AT FIRST GLANCE there is little to distinguish this manuscript, which contains Jerome's *Commentary on Daniel*, from many of the other copies of patristic commentaries in this exhibition.[1] A more careful examination of the text, however, reveals that only portions of Jerome's text have been included.[2] The amount of text omitted is extensive. Indeed, this manuscript can almost be better thought of as a collection of extracts from Jerome's work, than as a copy of his Commentary. The layout in this manuscript differs from that adopted in MS Riant 36, which contains three collections of extracts from works by a number of different authors (see cat.

no. 29). The layout in MS Riant 36 makes it immediately obvious that its scribes are copying selected passages from different sources. The abbreviation in fMS Lat 168, in contrast, was done silently; when the scribe finished a section of the text, he began his new section immediately, with no indication that he was leaving out a large part of the text.

It is not rare to find that a medieval manuscript does not contain a complete copy of any given text. In some cases, scribes were unable to find a complete copy, and were reduced to transcribing what was available. Manuscripts that were complete when they were made were often subsequently damaged in some way, resulting in the loss of sections of their text. Included in this exhibition are a number of manuscripts which now begin imperfectly (for example, MS Typ 205, cat. no. 21), or which survive in fragmentary condition (for example, cat. nos. 3, 7, 12, and 13). Indeed, the short length of this abbreviated version of Jerome's Commentary suggests that it may have originally been bound with another text, now lost. The manipulation of Jerome's text in the surviving portion of the manuscript, however, was almost certainly deliberate, and further study might determine why these passages were chosen, and others were omitted.

BIBLIOGRAPHY: Faye and Bond, 238.

NOTES:

[1]Franciscus Glorie, ed., *S. Hieronymi Presbyteri Opera. Pars 1. Opera Exegetica 5*. CC 75A (Turnholt 1964) 771-950; Bernard Lambert, O.S.B, *Bibliotheca hieronymiana manuscripta; la tradition manuscrite des oeuvres de saint Jerome,* Instrumenta patristica 4 (Steenbruges 1959) v. 2, no. 215, listing this manuscript, p. 142; *CPL* 588; Stegmüller 3358 (this manuscript not listed).

[2]For example, ff. 24-29 contain the following portions of the printed text: f. 24, line 3: ed., p. 865, line 140, followed by p. 886, line 553; f. 27v, line 16: ed., p. 900, line 890, followed by p. 914, line 1 ("De antichristo"); f. 28, line 13: ed., p. 915, line 42, followed by p. 917, line 2; f. 28, line 29: ed., p. 918, line 3, followed by p. 921, line 166; f. 28v, line 3: ed., p. 922, line 2, followed by p. 922, line 193; f. 28v, line 16: ed., p. 923, line 213, followed by p. 924, line 223; f. 28v, line 20: ed., p. 924, line 228, followed by p. 932, line 410; f. 29, line 12: ed., p. 934, line 1, followed by p. 935, line 471; f. 29, line 15: ed., p. 935, line 477, followed by p. 935, line 482.

28. Hugh of St. Victor and Bernard of Clairvaux, Monastic Sententiae; and Patristic Extracts

Southern or Central France s. XII² MS Lat 185

Parchment, ff. 110, 185 x 133 (136-134 x 90-86) mm. 21 long lines. Ruled lightly in lead, with the top 2 horizontal rules full across on most folios; double full-length vertical bounding lines. Prickings remain in top, and occasionally outer, margins.

1-13⁸ 14⁶.

Written on the top line in a twelfth-century minuscule by one scribe. Script is approaching gothic (feet used on all minims, forked ascenders, round 'r' and 'd' often used following round letters, round 's' sometimes used finally), but without letter-unions; occasional use of e-cedilla for 'ae.'

Two painted initials: f. 1, 5-line initial, extending into the upper margin, outlined in brown, with body of initial formed from a dragon, touched with green wash and red, which terminates in a spiral within the initial; and f. 41, 5-line pale yellow-brown initial infilled with a white-vine; both initials on blue grounds, outlined in red and decorated with red dots. 2- to 1-line alternately red and blue initials, some with simple pen flourishes in the other color. Red rubrics. Majuscules within the text daubed or stroked with red. Purchased March 18, 1941 (Treat Fund). Secundo folio: Tres sunt motus.

THE MANUSCRIPTS WHICH we have examined up to this point have all been copies of a single commentary. This manuscript, in contrast, which was written in southern or central France in the second half of the twelfth century, is a collection of numerous short texts by a number of different authors. Most of the manuscript is devoted to a collection of fifty-two monastic *sententiae*. The majority of the texts in the first group of thirty are by Hugh of St. Victor (d. 1141) and Bernard of Clairvaux (1090-1153).[1] The second group includes twenty-two *sententiae*, most of which are by Bernard.[2] The origin of fourteen of these texts is still undetermined. The manuscript concludes with a selection of patristic extracts, grouped together in sections headed by the author's name, followed by a short treatise on the Mass and other liturgical subjects.[3]

Monastic "sentences" are brief discussions of various topics, often moral in nature. They usually begin with a verse from scripture or a short summary or definition of the topic, which often consists of a numbered list, such as "The seven types of humility," "The seven deadly sins," or "The four kinds of monks," to choose a few examples from this manuscript. The length of each text varies; some are no more than a few comments on the topic, occupying half a page. Others are developed at greater length, and run for four pages, or occasionally even longer. A feature common to almost all of them is the frequent use of biblical citations to illustrate the point of the discussion. The origin of texts such as these is likely as miscellaneous as their contents. The majority, however, originated as sermons. Some may be summaries of a sermon noted down by someone who heard it preached. Others may represent notes compiled by the author of the sermon, either as an aid to his memory to use while he was preaching, or as a summary of a text he had already developed orally.[4]

Incipiunt dicta abbatis clareuallis.
Rex salomon fecit thronu de hebore
grande et uestiuit eu auro fuluo.
qui erat rotund' in parte priori et
erant due man' hinc et inde tenen
tes sedidio leones iuxta singtas man' erant
ad eu ascendendu sex gradus et sup illos xii.
leuncli. Nõ fuit tale op' in uniuisis regnis.
Solaris radius aliquando latet sub nebula: et de
lutuosis non nunquã elicitur preiosa marga
rita. Sic subiectis diuina teguntur misteria nec
alit legetur in sca ecctia: quia uideret quasi
ludibriu: immo fastidiosa quedã lenocinia. sa
lomon quinte etatis pacific' exprimit xpm:
tum nominis intpretacione. tã opis
celebritate. Qui pacificauit illã inexora
bile guerrã int dm et homines et anglos. Qui
fecit thronu: id est ppauit sibi beate ma
rie uirginis uteru ut eet in eo tanquã
sponsus in talamo. Salomon in templo rex
in solio: ds in celo. Vn cu eet rex in accubitu

The *sententiae* included here are arranged in no apparent order. The manuscript was not intended to be a systematic analysis of any particular topic or topics. It is simply a collection of useful texts. Collections of short discussions of various topics were also made in the twelfth-century schools. The scholastic "sentence" collection, in contrast with monastic collections, tends to be more systematically organized, and centers more often on doctrinal issues, or pastoral concerns. The scholastic sentence reflects its origin in the debates of the classroom, while the monastic collections are more closely tied to the sermon or homily.[5]

BIBLIOGRAPHY: Faye and Bond, 239; H. M. Rochais, O.S.B., "Inédits bernardins dans le manuscrit Harvard 185," *Analecta monastica. Textes et études sur la vie des moines au moyen âge* 6ᵉ série (Rome 1962) (= *Studia Anselmiana* 50) 53-175; J. Leclercq, O.S.B., "Manuscrits cisterciens" 165; H. M. Rochais, "Saint Bernard est-il l'auteur des sermons 40, 41 et 42 'De diversis'?," *Revue bénédictine* 72 (1962) 338, 345; J. Leclercq, "Saint Bernard écrivain d'après l'office de Saint Victor," *Revue bénédictine* 74 (1964) 160.

NOTES:

[1]H. M. Rochais, "Inédits bernardins dans le manuscrit Harvard 185," *Analecta monastica. Textes et études sur la vie des moines au moyen âge* 6ᵉ série (Rome 1962) (= *Studia Anselmiana* 50) 60-89, nos. 1-30, listing incipits and explicits, printing previously unpublished texts completely, and discussing the attribution of each item.

[2]Rochais, "Inédits," 89-169, nos. 31-52.

[3]Ff. 87-110v, see Rochais, "Inédits," 169, note 566, identifying some of the passages from Jerome on ff. 87v-92; remaining unidentified.

[4]Jean Leclercq, *The Love of Learning and the Desire for God: A Study of Monastic Culture*, Catharine Misrahi, tr.

(New York 1961) 208-11; Rochais, "Inédits bernardins," 56-7.

[5]On the contrast between the monastic and scholastic sentence collections, cf. C. H. Talbot, "The *Centum Sententiae* of Walter Daniel," *Sacris erudiri* 11 (1960) 277-278. The origin of the sentences in the schools is discussed in Smalley, *Study of the Bible*, 66-77. In general, see Jean Leclercq, "The Renewal of Theology," in *Renaissance and Renewal in the Twelfth Century*, R. L. Benson and Giles Constable, with Carol Lanham, eds. (Cambridge, Mass. 1982) 77-84.

29. Extracts from Patristic Authors and Others
Northern France s. XII⁴/⁴; s. XII³/⁴; Germany s. XII²   MS Riant 36

Parchment, ff. ii + 114 (incorrect foliation, cited, ff. 1-116, including two endleaves as ff. 1 and 2) + ii, 157-155 x 100-97 mm. Three independent manuscripts, now bound together.

I. ff. 3-54v: 1⁴ 2-7⁸; II. ff. 55-86v: 8-11⁸; III. ff. 87-116v: 12⁶ (all single; original structure uncertain) 13-15⁸.

I. ff. 3-54v: written space (120-119 x 65-62) mm. 30 long lines. Ruled in lead, with the top 2 and bottom 2 or 3 horizontal rules full across on some folios; single vertical bounding lines. Prickings in top and outer margins on most folios. Written above the top line in a small, careful, late twelfth-century minuscule; round 's,' 'd' and 'r' used frequently; all minims finished with feet turning upwards; forked or wedge-shaped ascenders. Major divisions within the text begin with 3- to 2-line orange-red initials, some with simple red pen decoration; other divisions indicated by simple paragraph marks. Red rubrics; majuscules within the text carefully filled with red. Secundo folio [f. 4]: Sother sedit annis.

II. ff. 55-86v: written space (117-116 x 78-72) mm. 29 long lines. Ruled lightly in lead with the top 2 and sometimes the bottom 2 horizontal rules full across; single full-length vertical bounding lines. Prickings on most folios in the three outer margins. Written above the top line in an informal, upright twelfth-century minuscule; 'ae' often written e-cedilla. Divisions within the text indicated by 4- to 1-line plain red initials. Red rubrics. Initials and rubrics are now very faded, with some recopied in a later hand; majuscules within the text crudely stroked with red on some pages by a later hand. Secundo folio [f. 56]: [concur]ritur plena est.

III. ff. 87-116v: written space (123-121 x 70-68) mm. 31 long lines. Ruled lightly in lead, occasionally with the top 2 or 3 and bottom 1 horizontal rules full across; single vertical bounding lines, full-length on some folios. Prickings in outer, and sometimes top and bottom margins. Written above the top line in an angular twelfth-century minuscule; 'ae' written as 'e' and e-cedilla. Sections within the text begin with 3- to 1-line green (some outlined in red) or red initials; the initial, f. 105, is blue. Majuscules within the text are sometimes daubed with red. Rubrics lacking. Secundo folio [f. 88]: Scimus in domo magna.

Belonged to Comte Paul Riant (1836-1888); his manuscripts given to Harvard in 1900 by J. Randolph Coolidge and Archibald Cary Coolidge.

IN STUDYING FORMAL MANUSCRIPTS such as Bibles, liturgical books and commentaries, it is easy to overlook the fact that every manuscript is unique. This is true in two senses. In the first place, even two copies of the same text are never exactly the same, simply because no scribe ever managed to copy his exemplar without introducing some changes, either intentionally or by error. Secondly, the texts included in any given manuscript directly reflect the needs of the original owner of the book. This aspect of the manuscript's uniqueness is particularly interesting in the case of manuscripts which contain a number of different texts, or extracts from various works. The manuscript we have just discussed, MS Lat 185 (cat. no. 28) includes a fairly diverse selection of monastic *sententiae* and extracts from patristic authors. It was likely compiled from a number of sources chosen to fit the needs of the person or community for which it was made. The manuscript shown here is an even better example of a book which was compiled to suit its owner; it is an example of a manuscript which was never intended to be copied more than once.

MS Riant 36 contains three physically discrete sections bound together. The evidence of the script of these sections, however, suggests an independent origin for each. The first two are likely French, but the third section was probably copied in Germany.[1] They are now bound in an eighteenth-century French binding. Although there is no way to determine at what date before the eighteenth century these three sections were combined to form a single manuscript, the evidence suggests that the second and third sections may have circulated together at an early date.[2]

A full analysis of the contents of the manuscript has not yet been made,[3] but an idea of the contents of this personal compendium can be gained from some of the texts included in the first two sections. In the first section, there are a number of extracts from letters attributed to Jerome, a long series of fairly brief extracts from Gregory's works, including many from the *Moralia in Job*, and selections from the sermons of Ivo of Chartres. The second section contains numerous letters attributed to Jerome, and some of Jerome's biblical prologues, including his prologues to the Pentateuch and the books of Kings, together with extracts from other fathers, and a selection of *sententiae* by Bernard. No obvious organizing principle emerges from reading through the extracts. Later writers contributed to the diversity of the contents, and added other texts, including poems by Hildebert of Lavardin, and astronomical notes.[4]

BIBLIOGRAPHY: De Ricci, 1004; L. de Germon and L. Polain, *Catalogue de la bibliothèque de feu M. le Comte Riant, deuxième partie* (Paris 1899) vol. 1, p. lii, no. 36; Mason Hammond, "A Description of a Manuscript of the Opuscula of St. Jerome in the Harvard Library," unpublished typescript and notes (Cambridge 1931) now Houghton bMS Lat 315(5 and 6); Mason Hammond, "Notes on Some Poems of Hildebert in a Harvard Manuscript, MS Riant 36" *Speculum* 7 (1932) 530-539 (with plate of ff. 80v-81).

NOTES:

[1]Cf. Mason Hammond, "Notes on Some Poems of Hildebert in a Harvard Manuscript, MS Riant 36," *Speculum* 7 (1932) 530, suggesting that the manuscript may have been made near Cambrai, since it contains an eighteenth-century ex-libris note on f. 4 from the Abbey of St. Sepulchre in Cambrai, and describing the hands in all three sections as similar. I would argue, however, that the script in the last section of the manuscript is markedly different from that in the other two sections.

[2]As noted previously by Mason Hammond in "A Description of a Manuscript of the Opuscula of St. Jerome in the Harvard Library" (unpublished typescript) now Houghton bMS Lat 315(5), 23, the script and text on f. 91v of the third section and f. 85v, a leaf with added text in the second section, are related; the script used to copy the texts added on ff. 82-84 of the second section is also similar to the type of script used in the third section.

[3]Contents are partially listed by Mason Hammond in his unpublished description of the manuscript, see note 2 above.

[4]See Hammond, "Notes on Some Poems of Hildebert in a Harvard Manuscript," 530-539.

Introduction

THE ORDINARY GLOSS on the Bible consists of explanatory notes extracted from patristic and medieval commentaries, which were collected together and arranged around the biblical text, so that one could read both the Scriptures and the most important commentaries simultaneously. Equipped with a Bible and its Gloss, a reader had access to all of the most important interpretations on any given book of the Bible in one convenient compendium. The Gloss made the time-consuming process of searching through long commentaries and comparing their texts unnecessary. It also provided access to texts that were often difficult to find and expensive to copy.

The practice of adding notes in the margins of books is a very old one, and one which certainly continues today. It can be seen in medieval manuscripts of many types other than the Bible, including grammars, law books and classical texts (see cat. no. 30). The Ordinary Gloss on the Bible, however, is more than a collection of personal notes; it is a collection compiled by famous teachers, which was accepted as the standard commentary on the Bible, reproduced in numerous, widely disseminated copies. The Gloss originated in the teaching of the masters of the cathedral school at Laon in the late eleventh and early twelfth centuries, especially Anselm of Laon (d. 1117) and his brother Ralph (d. 1133), and their pupils, including Gilbert the Universal (d. 1134) and others whose names are now unknown. The work of compiling the Gloss was a long process, which proceeded book by book. The Gloss on most of the biblical books was probably substantially complete by c. 1130-1150, and gradually, from about the middle of the century, it seems to have been increasingly accepted as a standard text, which circulated with some degree of uniformity.[1]

The Psalms and the Pauline Epistles were two of the earliest groups of biblical books to be glossed at Laon, and they were the only texts in the Ordinary Gloss that were extensively revised during the twelfth century. The first major revision was the work of Gilbert de la Porrée (c. 1080-1154), a student at Laon under Anselm and Ralph. He combined Anselm's short marginal and interlinear glosses into continuous commentaries on the Psalms and Pauline Epistles; these commentaries were probably both complete by c. 1130 (see cat. nos. 35 and 36).[2] Peter Lombard (d. 1160) in turn, composed an expanded version of Gilbert's Commentaries on these books; although written earlier, these commentaries circulated for the most part only after his death in 1160.[3] The earlier version of the Ordinary Gloss on both these books continued to be used throughout the twelfth century (see cat. no. 31), but the newer versions were often preferred. Gilbert and Peter Lombard were both famous teachers, and the use of the Ordinary Gloss in their writings and lectures may have been instrumental in ensuring its acceptance as the standard commentary in the theology schools of Paris. By the later decades of the twelfth century, the biblical commentaries of masters such as Peter Comestor (d. ca. 1178), Peter the Chanter (d. 1197), and Stephen Langton (d. 1228), who left the schools in 1206, are commentaries on the Bible and its accompanying Gloss.[4]

The task of copying the biblical text and the glosses on the same page was a particularly challenging one. Over the course of the twelfth century, scribes adopted different solutions to the problem. The changing layout of Glossed Bibles, as Christopher de Hamel has shown in his recent book, to some extent reflects the increasing standardization of the text.[5] The scribes of the earliest manuscripts seem to have copied the complete text of the book of the Bible first, in a narrow column running down the center of the page; comments were then added in the margins and between the lines. This method had the advantage of allowing plenty of space for changes and additions even after the manuscript was complete.

From the second quarter of the twelfth century, perhaps from c. 1130, the biblical text and the glosses were copied together, page by page, rather than as part of a two-step process. The scribe first copied the biblical text in a column in the center of the page as before. In this case, however, he adjusted the amount of biblical text he wished to place on the page, depending on the length and number of glosses, by varying the width of the column, and sometimes the numbers of lines (see cat. nos. 31 and 32). He then added the glosses in the empty spaces on either side of the biblical text, before proceeding to the next page, and beginning the process again.

The third stage in the development of the layout of Glossed Bibles was reached with the adoption of the "alternate-line" format, which Dr. de Hamel has argued was first used in books copied in Paris around 1160. The scribe copied the text and the glosses on the same set of ruled lines, using every line for the glosses, and alternate lines for the biblical text. In order to minimize the amount of empty space even further, scribes adjusted the width of the column of biblical text even on a single page, thus allowing the glosses to be fitted neatly into the remaining space (see cat. no. 37). The three-column format, with a central column of biblical text flanked on both sides by columns of Gloss, is often abandoned in these manuscripts; the number of columns allotted to either the text or the Gloss is adjusted depending on the content. The layouts used in manuscripts of the two expanded versions of the Gloss on the Pauline Epistles and the Psalter by Gilbert de la Porrée (see cat. nos. 35 and 36) and Peter Lombard form an interesting link between the earlier formats, and the appearance of this "alternate-line" format in manuscripts of the other books of the Bible.

These methods of copying Glossed Bibles represent three progressively more sophisticated approaches to the task, which were adopted over the course of the twelfth century. Care should be taken, however, not to view this schema as strictly a chronological one. Glossed Bibles copied according to the "alternate-line" format, for example, do not appear before c. 1160; nonetheless, as demonstrated by two of the manuscripts included here (cat. nos. 33 and 34), manuscripts continued to be copied according to "older" methods.

NOTES:

[1]De Hamel, *Glossed Books,* 1-5; de Hamel's summary of the history of the Gloss overemphasizes the degree of standardization reached by c. 1130; cf. Smalley, *Study of the Bible,* 46-66, and Guy Lobrichon, "Une nouveauté: les gloses de la Bible," *Le Moyen Age et la Bible,* P. Riché and G. Lobrichon, eds., Bible de tous les Temps 4 (Paris 1984) 103-111; Lobrichon in particular gives a more balanced account of how long the process of "standardization" took.

[2]De Hamel, *Glossed Books,* 4-7 and 18-20, and works cited there.

[3]*Ibid.,* 7-9; Smalley, *Study of the Bible,* 64.

[4]Smalley, *Study of the Bible,* 64-65, and 216-219; Lobrichon, "Les gloses de la Bible," 109-110.

[5]The following discussion of the format of Glossed Bible is based on de Hamel, *Glossed Books,* chapter 2, "The layout of the Pages," 14-27.

30. Priscian, Institutiones grammaticae
France s. XII[2/4]   MS Lat 44

Parchment, ff. ii + 213 + ii, 220 x 121[1] (text: 175-170 x 80-75; text and gloss: 203-186 x 126-105) mm. 35-33 long lines of text, with glosses in the unruled space in the outer margin; glosses also copied between the lines and in the other margins on some folios. Ruled in hard point (except quire 5, beginning f. 31, in lead), with the top 1 or 2 and bottom 1 or 2 horizontal rules full across; double full-length vertical bounding lines. Prickings in the three outer margins on most folios.

1[8] (-1 and 8, following f. 6, with loss of text) 2-13[8] 14[6] 15-18[8] 19[8] (3, f. 143 and 6, f. 146, are single) 20-22[8] 23[8] (-2, following f. 173, with no loss of text) 24-27[8] 28[8] (-1, 2, 3, and 6, 7, 8, before and after ff. 212-213, a conjugate pair, with loss of text). Quires signed with small roman numerals in ink, middle, lower margin, verso of last leaf.

Written above the top ruled line in a twelfth-century minuscule by at least 4 scribes; 'ae' usually written e-cedilla; ampersand used internally as an abbreviation for 'et.'

Five- to 2-line initials in red or brown ink, usually plain, but some with decorative void spaces within the initial, used at the beginnings of the books. Secondary divisions indicated by 2- to 1-line initials. Headings in display capitals, brown ink (often omitted). Purchased from Quaritch, January 2, 1897 (Charles Minot fund). Secundo folio: (now f. 1) esse inuentionibus.

PRISCIAN'S *Institutiones Grammaticae,* written in the early sixth century, was a standard school text during the Middle Ages. In the first sixteen books, Priscian discusses the parts of speech at great length, illustrated by numerous examples, many taken from classical authors. The remaining two books discuss syntax. By the twelfth century most copies of this text include only the first sixteen books, known as the "Priscianus maior"; the last two books circulated separately.[2] Our manuscript, which begins and ends imperfectly, was most likely a copy of books 1-16, even though the scribe absent-mindedly included books 17 and 18 in the table of contents.[3]

The most noteworthy feature of the twelfth-century copy of Priscian's grammar exhibited here, is the extensive notes written in the margins and between the lines in a number of different hands. Numerous commentaries were composed during the Middle Ages to explain Priscian's text.[4] These explanations were either copied as separate treatises, or, as in this manuscript, added in the margins of a copy of Priscian. The marginal notes in our manuscript have not been identified with any known commentary.[5] It is likely that they should not be thought of as a formal commentary, circulating in multiple copies, at all, but rather as notes added by the book's users throughout much of its history, comparable to the highlights, underlinings, marginal scribbles, etc., added by students today to their textbooks.

Informal glosses such as these, as well as more standardized commentaries, were added to school texts from a very early time. Classical texts and treatises on law were also glossed. The development of the Ordinary Gloss on the Bible, which consists of extracts from Patristic and early medieval commentaries, written in the margins of copies of the text of the Bible and between the lines of the biblical text, should be seen in the context of this long tradition. Early glosses on the Bible were as informal as the notes added in this copy of Priscian, and the standardization of the Gloss on the various books of the Bible, compiled mostly by Anselm and Ralph and their pupils at Laon in the late eleventh and early twelfth centuries, was a long and gradual process.

BIBLIOGRAPHY: De Ricci, 981; listed in Margaret Gibson, "Priscian, 'Institutiones Grammaticae': A Handlist of Manuscripts," *Scriptorium* 26 (1972) 108; briefly described in: Marina Passalacqua, *I codici di Prisciano*, Sussidi Eruditi 29 (Rome 1978) 44, no. *94; G. L. Bursill-Hall, *A Census of Medieval Latin Grammatical Manuscripts*. Grammatica Speculativa 4 (Stuttgart-Bad Canstatt 1981) 93, no. 116.1; and Guglielmo Ballaira, *Per il catalogo dei codici di Prisciano* (Turin 1982) 227, no. *94.

NOTES:

[1]Note: physical description does not apply to quire 14, ff. 103-108v, which was added to the manuscript in the second half of the twelfth century: written space (176-172 x 80-71) mm. 35 long lines. Ruled in lead, with the top 2 and bottom 2 horizontal rules full across; double full-length vertical bounding lines. Prickings in the three outer margins.

[2]Margaret Gibson, "Priscian, 'Institutiones Grammaticae': A Handlist of Manuscripts," *Scriptorium* 26 (1972) 105.

[3]M. Hertz, ed., *Prsciani grammatici Caesariensis institutionum grammaticarum libri XVIII.* in H. Keil, *Grammatici latini* (Leipzig 1855 and 1859) vols. 2 and 3, with book 16 ending on p. 105; first quire is lacking its first and last leaves, so the text begins imperfectly in the dedicatory epistle [ed., 2:2, line 14], and continues through f. 6v, book 1.26 [ed., 2:20, line 16]; resumes on f. 7, book 1.31

[ed., 2:23, line 21], continuing through f. 211v, book 14.32 [ed., 3:40, line 18]. Last quire missing all but the middle bifolium, so that the text resumes on f. 212, book 14.45 [ed., 3:49, line 10], and continues through f. 213v, book 14.52 [ed., 3:55, line 21], where it breaks off incomplete.

[4]See R. W. Hunt, *The History of Grammar in the Middle Ages; Collected Papers*, G. L. Bursill-Hall, ed., in Amsterdam Studies in the Theory and History of Linguistic Science, series 3, vol. 5 (Amsterdam 1980).

[5]The glosses were examined by R. W. Hunt on a visit to the library, who noted that he knew of no source; Beverly Kienzle, currently researching the glosses in the manuscript, has observed that some of the glosses use the first person, and that others include references to Lanfranc.

31. Psalms with the Ordinary Gloss
Italy (Tuscany) s. XII² MS Typ 260

Parchment, ff. i + 235 (foliated in ink, top outer corner, 1-93; continued, 94-235, in pencil, bottom, inside corner) + i, 280 x 183 mm.; ruled space, text and gloss: 173-172 x 156-154 mm. Biblical text, written space: (174-173 x 61-60) mm.; copied in one central column of 18 lines, ruled in hard point with the top and bottom horizontal rules full across; double full-length vertical bounding lines. Gloss, written in a smaller script, is arranged in 2 columns flanking the text and between the lines; number of lines varies, up to 42 lines; copied on horizontal rules added as needed in brown crayon; full-length single vertical bounding lines in hard point. Prickings for vertical bounding lines (text and gloss) only remain, top and bottom margins.

1⁸ (+ 1, singleton with painted initial) 2-29⁸ 30² (singletons; original structure uncertain, possibly quire of 4, with 3 and 4 cancelled; no loss of text). Horizontal catchwords, copied at the bottom edge or slightly above, under the column of biblical text (some excised).

Text written above the top line in a rounded Italian "reformed" twelfth-century minuscule; uncial letterforms used for display script; gloss, also beginning above the top line, written in a smaller, more prickly hand.

One full page brushed-gold initial, f. 1v (f. 1 is blank), outlined in orange, with shaft filled with blue, green and orange patterns in the geometric style, ending in interlace, and with a white-vine scroll within the initial, shaded in green and orange on deep blue; on a deep-blue rectangular ground, decorated with small red and white dots, framed in the geometric style and outlined in brushed gold; opening words of the text copied below the initial in white. Similar 3- to 5-line initials at the beginning of the psalms marking the liturgical divisions; initial, f. 31 (psalm 26) with grotesque of a horned bird extending from the initial. Remaining psalms begin with 2- to 3-line yellow initials infilled with simple white-vine scrolls or infrequently, with birds, on blue grounds following the shape of the initial, outlined in red, or with 2- to 4-line red initials, with decorative void spaces within the initials. Verses of the psalms begin with 1-line orange-red initials; orange-red rubrics. Purchased by Philip Hofer from Maggs in 1952. Deposited by Hofer in the library, 1 January 1967; accession record: *68M-150(10). Hofer bequest, 1984. Secundo folio: [text] Qui non abiit; [Gloss] Non abiit a deo.

THIS MANUSCRIPT CONTAINS the Psalms with the Ordinary Gloss, followed by the Old Testament canticles and the Athanasian Creed, also with glosses.[1] The Gloss on the psalms was compiled at the schools of Laon, probably by Anselm of Laon (d. 1117), in the late eleventh or early twelfth century. In the second half of the twelfth century, an expanded version of Anselm's Gloss compiled by Gilbert de la Porrée (c. 1080-1154), often replaced the earlier text (see cat. no. 36). Subsequently, a third version of the Gloss on the Psalms was compiled by Peter Lombard (c. 1100-1160). These later commentaries never completely replaced Anselm's Gloss, however, as witnessed by this copy, which was written and decorated in Tuscany in the second half of the twelfth century.[2]

The format of this manuscript is extremely conservative; copies of this text produced during the first half of the twelfth century were organized in the same manner.[3] The biblical text is copied in a large script in a single column running down the center of the page. The number of lines and the width of the column are the same throughout the manuscript. The glosses are copied in a smaller script, in two columns on either side of the biblical text, and between the lines. The scribe copied the biblical text on guidelines made by drawing impressions in the surface

84

of the parchment with a pointed instrument, such as a stylus. Two vertical lines on either side of the text, and single vertical lines in the far inside and outside margins next to the glosses, were also made in this manner. Since the space reserved for the biblical text is the same throughout the manuscript, it is likely that these rulings were completed before the manuscript was written.[4] The amount of Gloss on each page, in contrast, varies, and the scribe added lines in brown crayon for the glosses as needed.

This is a handsome manuscript, which begins on f. 1v with a full-page painted frontispiece. Smaller painted initials are used at the traditional liturgical divisions of the psalter, marking the psalms to be read at Matins throughout the week, beginning on Sunday with the first psalm, and then continuing through the week with psalms 26 (Monday), 38 (Tuesday), 52 (Wednesday), 68 (Thursday), 80 (Friday), and 97 (Saturday); psalm 109, the beginning of the cycle of psalms read at Vespers also begins with a painted initial.[5]

BIBLIOGRAPHY: Faye and Bond, 274; *Harvard Cat.* (1955) p. 12, no. 14 and plate 6 (reproducing f. 1v); Knut Berg, *Studies in Tuscan Twelfth-Century Illumination* (Oslo 1968) 230, cat. no. 11, and text, p. 174; E. B. Garrison, *Studies in the History of Mediaeval Italian Painting, I-IV* (Florence 1953-1962) III:160ff.

NOTES:
[1]Text as follows: ff. 1-220v Psalms with the Glossa Ordinaria, Stegmüller 11801; this manuscript lacks most of the introductory glosses listed by Stegmüller; ff. 220v-231v Old Testament Canticles with glosses, cf. Stegmüller 11801,1-6; ff. 232-235v Athanasian creed with glosses.

[2]See Knut Berg, *Studies in Tuscan Twelfth-Century Illumination* (Oslo 1968) p. 230, cat. no. 11, and text, p. 174, and more generally, 168-174; Berg has grouped it together with a number of other manuscripts which are decorated in a style which he designates the "Florentine-Pisan" school; he warns, however, that this style was popular throughout Tuscany in the second half of the twelfth cen-

tury, and thus cannot be used to localize the manuscripts in this group more exactly.

[3]See de Hamel, *Glossed Books*, 15-17 describing this early form of layout, and 26, noting that it continued in use in copies of the Psalms with the Anselmian Gloss at least until the end of the century.

[4]Prickings for the vertical bounding lines remain in the top and bottom margins. It is almost certain that the manuscript once included prickings in the outer margin for the biblical text, but these have been trimmed.

[5]Ff. 1v, 31, 49v, 68, 90, 117v, 142v, 166v.

32.   Leviticus with the Ordinary Gloss
Paris or Germany(?) s. XII^med   fMS Typ 204

Parchment (fuzzy), ff. i + 74 (foliated 1-73; f. 74, blank, lifted pastedown, conjoint with f. 73), 265 x 180 mm., ruled space, text and gloss: 178-176 x 146-139 mm. Prickings in the outer, top and bottom margins for a central column of biblical text of 15 lines, bounded on the inside and outside by double full-length vertical bounding lines; the width and number of lines of the column of biblical text actually varies from page to page, depending on ratio of text to gloss. Biblical text, written space (178-176 x 76-24) mm.; ruled in lead, with one

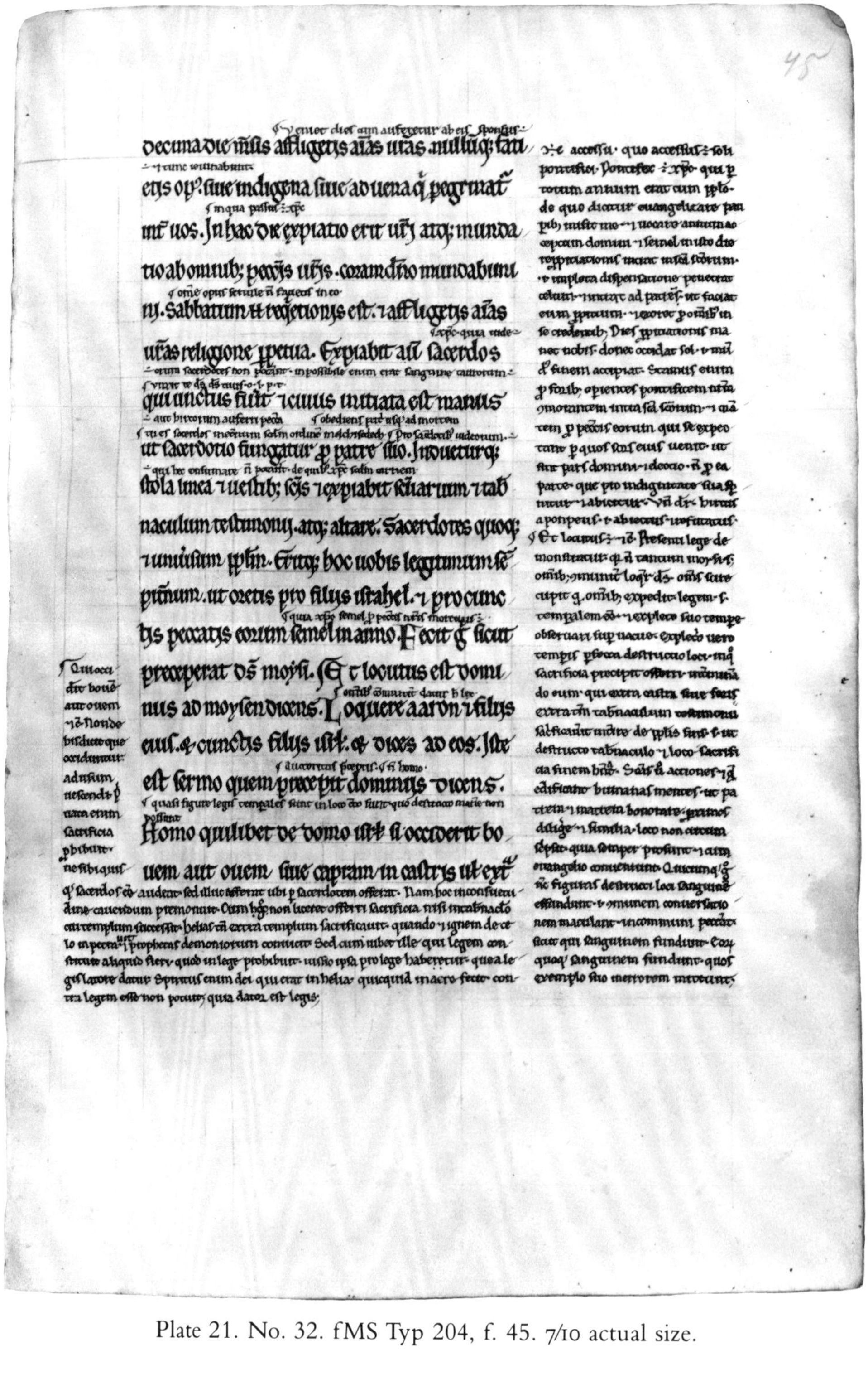

Plate 21. No. 32. fMS Typ 204, f. 45. 7/10 actual size.

column of 20-15 lines. Gloss, copied in a smaller script, is usually arranged in columns flanking the biblical text and between the lines; ruling for gloss, in lead, was done page by page, with no prickings, independently of the ruling for the biblical text; single full-length vertical bounding lines; number of lines varies from 38 to 41.

1-9⁸ 10² (conjugate pair; 2, f. 74, lifted pastedown). Signed, middle, bottom edge, verso of last leaf, in small roman numerals with decorative flourishes (mostly cut away).

Biblical text written above the top line in a formal twelfth-century minuscule; ductus and many of the letter forms are close to gothic, but letter unions are not used; e-cedilla is occasionally used for 'ae' (cf. f. 11, second line from bottom). Gloss, also beginning above the top line, copied in a smaller, but very similar script.

One bright orange-yellow initial, equivalent to 4-lines of text, outlined in orange, with the shaft and bow infilled with geometric-style interlace in shades of dark green and orange with yellow highlights, on a stepped-ground of maroon and blue, with yellow dots; infilled with a leafy white vine, shaded with red and yellow, on blue; the opening word of the text is completed in yellow capitals, arranged vertically on a narrow maroon rectangle alongside the initial. Divisions within the text indicated by plain initials, alternately red and blue. Manuscript was acquired from Admont, probably in 1934, by E. P. Goldschmidt.¹ Purchased by Philip Hofer from Goldschmidt in 1935; presented to the library by Hofer, September 15, 1955, "In recognition of the outstanding services of William A. Jackson." Accession record: *55M-17. Secundo folio: [gloss] [obtule]rant sed que; [text] Vocauit autem moysen.

THIS COPY OF LEVITICUS with the Ordinary Gloss² belonged to the Benedictine Abbey of St. Blaise at Admont, Styria.³ The Abbey of St. Blaise was built by Archbishop Gebhard in 1074, and colonized by the Abbey of St. Peter at Salzburg.⁴ Although the manuscript's presence at Admont is well documented, it may have been copied in Paris and brought to Admont during the abbacy of Gottfried (1138-65), who was known as a patron of learning with connections to the Paris schools.⁵ Our manuscript is still in its original binding, made of brown leather decorated with stamped impressions of pictures and decorative patterns, which completely cover its front and back covers. The question of where this manuscript and a group of related manuscripts with similar bindings, were copied, has been the subject of considerable scholarly debate.⁶ The arguments are too lengthy to review in detail here, but it may be noted that accepting a Parisian provenance means that one must argue that a group of books copied and decorated in different styles, originated in the same location, primarily on the basis of the similarity of their bindings.⁷ Dr. de Hamel has argued that the early ownership of these books, as well as the fact that they are primarily copies of books of the Bible with the Gloss, support a Parisian provenance.⁸ However, although it is certainly possible that these books were copied and bound in Paris, the evidence is not conclusive, and we still know too little about Parisian book production during the twelfth century to definitively decide the question.⁹

The layout used in this manuscript is an interesting variation on the layout used for many glossed books copied around the middle of the twelfth century. If the scribe had followed the prickings in the top, bottom and outer margins, the manuscript would have been ruled for a column of biblical text of fifteen lines running down the center of each page. For the most part, however, the scribe ignored the prickings, and carefully adjusted the amount of text included on each page by varying both the width of the biblical text and the number of lines, depending on the length and number of the glosses. The glosses were then copied in a smaller script in columns on either side of the text and between the lines. While copying this manuscript, the scribe had to stop before he began each new page, assess the ratio of text to gloss, and rule the page accordingly before he proceeded with his copying. This time-consuming process did produce a book which uses the available space efficiently. It also suggests that the scribe was likely following his exemplar very carefully — it certainly would have made his task easier — and is therefore an indication that he was treating the Ordinary Gloss on this book of the Bible, at least to some extent, as a standard, fixed text.

BIBLIOGRAPHY: De Ricci, 1693 (= New York, Collection of Philip Hofer, MS 4); Faye and Bond, 270; P. Buberl, *Die illuminierte Handschriften in Steiermark; 1. Die Stiftsbibliotheken zu Admont und Vorau*. Beschreibendes Verzeichnis der Illuminierten Handschriften in Österreich 4 (Leipzig 1911) 158, no. 195 [347]; G. D. Hobson, *English Binding before 1500* (Cambridge 1929) app. B, no. 36 and plate 16; G. D. Hobson, "Further Notes on Romanesque Bindings," *The Library*, 4th series, 15 (1935) app. A, p. 198, no. 136 and app. B, p. 205; *Harvard Cat.* (1955) 12, no. 19 (no plate); Harvard College Library, *The Houghton Library 1942-1967. A Selection of Books and Manuscripts in Harvard Collections* (Cambridge, Mass. 1967) p. 176 (plate, reproducing binding); de Hamel, *Glossed Books*, 66, 71, and 75.

NOTES:

[1] Cf. the sales catalogue, New York, Parke Bernet, October 29, 1951, lot 111, Glossed John, now Oxford, Bodleian Library, Broxbourne Library [formerly Admont MS 568; Hobson no. 39], citing portions of letters from Goldschmidt to Mr. Wilmerding discussing the sale of the Glossed John, as well as the Admont manuscript which is now fMS Typ 204.

[2] Marginal and interlinear glosses correspond in content with those listed in Stegmüller 11783 (Leviticus with Glossa Ordinaria), although they appear in a different order; later hand added small minuscule letters before three glosses on f. 1rv, indicating that the glosses now 3rd, 2nd and 6th, should be 1st, 2nd, and 3rd.

[3] Formerly Admont MS 347; ff. 2 and 73, round library stamp, "Bibliotheca Admontensis," with coat-of-arms; description in German, handwritten on paper, recording the manuscript as no. 347, glued on verso of front endleaf.

[4] L. H. Cottineau, *Répertoire topo-bibliographique des abbayes et prieures* (Mâcon 1935) 20-21, with lengthy bibliography.

[5] E. Ph. Goldschmidt, "Austrian Monastic Libraries," *The Library* 4th series, 25 (1945) 61-2; and de Hamel, *Glossed Books*, 76, discussing 3 manuscripts from Admont.

[6] Bound in the shop which Hobson called the Rowel Spur Binder; see G. D. Hobson, *English Binding before 1500* (Cambridge 1929) listing this manuscript as Admont MS 347, appendix B, no. 36, plate 16, and "Further Notes on Romanesque Bindings," *The Library* 4th series, 15 (1935) 161-211, listing this manuscript, as Admont MS 347, appendix A, p. 198, no. 36, and appendix B, p. 205, ascrib-

ing the binding to Paris. Schilling noted that this binder and the binder Hobson called Prince Henry's First Binder, should be considered as one; see R. Schilling, "Neue romanische Bucheinbände; 2. Engelberg," *Jahrbuch der Einbandkunst* 3-4 (1929/30) 15-31; the manuscripts in this combined group are listed by de Hamel, *Glossed Books*, 71; de Hamel argues for a Parisian provenance. Ilse Schunke in "Die romanischen Einbände in Deutschland," *Festschrift Ernst Kyriss* (Stuttgart 1961) 17-32, suggested a German provenance for some of the manuscripts ascribed to Paris by Hobson and others; however, she believed that the "Rowel Spur Binder," (here called "Der Meister des deutschen Klerus") was working in Paris; see p. 18, note 3 (listing fMS Typ 204, as Hobson 36), and 21-22.

[7] The major initial in our manuscript, for example, was possibly added in Admont; it shows the influence of Italian manuscripts; Paul Buberl, *Die Illuminierten Handschriften in Steiermark; 1. Die Stiftsbibliotheken zu Admont und Vorau*. Beschreibendes Verzeichnis der Illuminierten Handschriften in Österreich 4 (Leipzig 1911), p. 158, no. 195 [347], who considered the manuscript to be Austrian, s. XIII, but compares the initial style to two earlier Italian manuscripts.

[8] De Hamel, *Glossed Books*, 64-86.

[9] One wonders if binders could have been itinerant, or binders' tools disseminated more widely than has previously been suggested; certainly the ill-assembled patterns on some of these books suggest that the person using the tools no longer understood their original purpose.

33. Gospel of John with the Ordinary Gloss
Italy (Morimondo) s. XII[4/4]   MS Richardson 2

Parchment (stiff), ff. i + 82 (modern foliation 1-83 includes f. 1, original parchment endleaf) + i, 228 x 148 mm., written space, text and gloss (approximately 160-155 x 135-127) mm. Biblical text is copied in a central column, with the size of the written space adjusted depending on the ratio of text to gloss, ranging from (147 x 57) mm., when it is copied between the vertical bounding lines, to (150 x 130) mm., when it extends full across the page; width of the column can vary on a single page; 16 lines; ruled in hard point, ff. 1-25v, and thereafter in lead, with the top and bottom horizontal rules full across, and with double full-length vertical bounding lines. Gloss is copied in a smaller script, with roughly 2 lines of gloss per each line of text, arranged in columns flanking the biblical text, or in blocks surrounded by the biblical text; ruled in brown crayon; on some folios columns of gloss are subdivided (cf. f. 4rv). Prickings top, bottom, and outer margins for biblical text only.

1[8] (beginning f. 2; f. 1, an endleaf) 2-10[8] 11[2] (conjugate pair). Each quire is signed with a letter, flourished on all sides, center, lower margin, on the verso of the last leaf; horizontal catchwords, lower, inside margin, verso of last leaf, all enclosed by a paragraph sign (except quire 10, f. 81v).

Text written above the top line in an upright, rounded twelfth-century minuscule, with marked contrast between thick and thin strokes; adjacent round letters usually touch; 'ae' occasionally represented by e-cedilla; gloss is copied above the top line in a smaller, more compressed script, using similar letter forms.

Blank spaces remain for a 6- and 9-line initial on ff. 2 and 4; very bright orange used for rubrics. Text was originally undivided; divisions for modern chapters added: 1-line orange initials within the text, with marginal roman numerals; and, sporadically, in an earlier hand, marked in the text by a simple angle-bracket in brown, and marginal roman numerals enclosed by a paragraph sign. Purchased from Martini by William King Richardson. His bequest to Harvard, March 1, 1951. Accession record: *50M-257. Secundo folio: quod ubi dominus.

THE TWELFTH-CENTURY LIBRARY catalogue from Morimondo in fMS Typ 223 (see cat. nos. 1 and 10), notes that the monastery owned a glossed copy of the Gospel of John. By the early thirteenth century, Morimondo had acquired a second copy, and the entry, modified a little later by another writer, reads: "Euangelium iohannis glosatum duo uolumina."[1] One of these two copies can almost certainly be identified with the manuscript shown here.[2] It includes a thirteenth-century note of ownership on f. 1v, which states, "This book belongs to St. Mary of Morimondo, which is near Pavia," and a similar note in a later hand on f. 2.[3] The manuscript was heavily used, and numerous marginal notes can still be discerned, although many are now very faint and virtually illegible.

The manuscript can be dated to the later part of the twelfth century on the basis of its script. The basic layout of the biblical text and the Gloss on the opening leaves, ff. 2-9v, however, is as conservative as the one we saw used in MS Typ 260 (see cat. no. 31). The leaves were first pricked for sixteen widely spaced lines, used to draw the horizontal rules for the biblical text. The glosses, arranged in columns on either side of the text, were copied in a smaller script on lines added by the scribe as they were needed. The text and Gloss were copied in different colors of ink; the lines for the text were ruled in hard point, and those for the gloss in lead. This layout is modified on ff. 10-25v, where the scribe changes the size of the

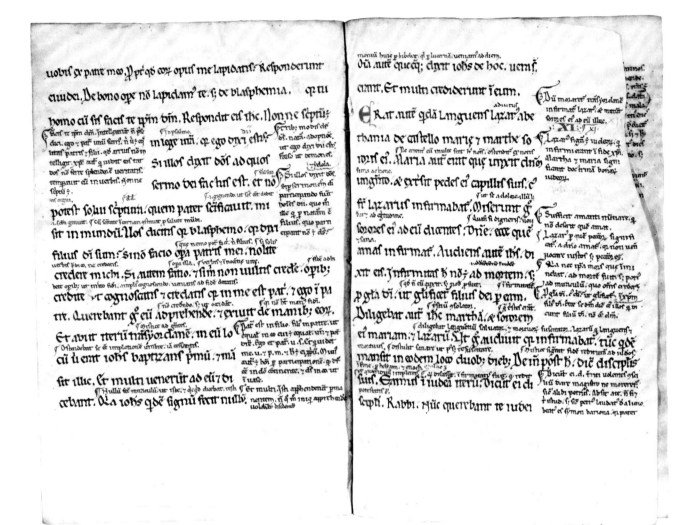

Plate 22. No. 33. MS Richardson 2, ff. 47v–48. 4/5 actual size.

central column of biblical text from page to page to accommodate the varying amount of Gloss. These leaves were ruled in the same manner as the earliest section of the manuscript, but the text and the glosses were copied in the same color of ink.

A more sophisticated layout is adopted in the last section, beginning on f. 26. On these pages, the biblical text often extends past the vertical bounding lines, and the Gloss often encroaches on the area usually reserved for the text of the Bible. Moreover, the width of the column of text not only varies from page to page, but it also changes in the course of a single page, allowing the scribe to insert the glosses in small blocks in the appropriate places. These pages are similar in appearance to the pages laid out according to the "alternate-line" format, with their closely interwoven blocks of text and Gloss (see cat. no. 37). In this manuscript, however, the ruling for the text and the Gloss was still added in two separate steps.[4] On these folios, the scribe used lead to rule both the text and the Gloss, and copied them both in the same color of ink. The increasing sophistication of the layout adopted by this scribe as he progresses through the manuscript, may simply have been the result of growing confidence and experience. It might also suggest that the scribe had access to a number of manuscripts, laid-out according to different formats, which he either used as his exemplars, or simply consulted as models for the format of his text.

BIBLIOGRAPHY: De Ricci, 956 (= Boston, Library of William King Richardson, MS 2); Faye and Bond, 246.

NOTES:
[1]Leclercq, "Manuscrits cisterciens," 179, no. 36.
[2]John with Glossa Ordinaria; Stegmüller 11830.
[3]F. 1v, in a thirteenth-century hand, "Iste liber est sancte marie de Morimundo quod est prope Ticinum"; f. 2, in a later hand, "Liber sancte marie de morimondo mediolanensis dyocesis ordine cisterciensis numero C."

[4]De Hamel, *Glossed Books*, 24-26; cf. esp. p. 25, n. 63, citing examples of manuscripts which combine different formats within one volume, and a manuscript, copied before 1164-8, in which the width of the biblical text changes within a single page, although the text and the Gloss are still ruled independently.

34.   Numbers with the Ordinary Gloss
Italy s. XII$^{3/4}$ MS Lat 334

Parchment, ff. i + 108 (correctly foliated, bottom, inside margin, in pencil, cited; incorrectly foliated, top outer corner in pencil, 1-106) + ii, 214 x c.150 mm., written space, text and gloss (173-142 x 130-125) mm. Number of lines and layout vary, with 3, 2, or 1 columns, depending on ratio of text to gloss: biblical text in the central column, flanked by columns of gloss; a broad column of text on the inside, with a single column of gloss on the outside; or one column of text, copied in long lines, without gloss or interrupted by small blocks of gloss. Written space, text, varies from (153-130 x 70-31) mm., with 11-19 lines, to (145 x 125) mm., with 25 lines on pages without gloss. Gloss is copied in a smaller script so that 2 to 3 lines of gloss are equivalent to 1 line of text, with up to 37-38 lines. Ruled very lightly in hard point or brown crayon for text and gloss; text and gloss were ruled independently, in two steps. Prickings (often cut away), in the three outer margins, intended for pages with a central column of biblical text of 14 lines, bounded on both sides by double vertical bounding lines, and flanked by columns of gloss on the inside and outside, bounded by single vertical bounding lines.

Text and gloss both written above the top line in a twelfth-century minuscule, approaching gothic, but lacking letter unions, and with occasional use of e-cedilla for 'ae'; the gloss is copied in a smaller script using similar letter forms; "qui" abbreviated in the Italian manner.

1^2 (conjugate pair) $2\text{-}14^8$ 15^2 (ff. 107-108, blank leaves, glued to quire 14). Horizontal catchword, very bottom, inside margin, quire 2, f. 10v.

Blank space remains for 1- to 2-line initial at the beginning of the biblical text, f. 3. Presented by Charles R. Blyth of Cambridge, Massachusetts, August 28, 1972. Accession record: ★72M-6. Secundo folio: omnes tamen intra trinitatis.

THIS COPY OF NUMBERS with the Ordinary Gloss[1] and MS Richardson 2, the Glossed John from Morimondo (see cat. no. 33), may serve as useful reminders of the fact that some glossed books of the Bible were unpretentious manuscripts, designed primarily for study. Neither manuscript is elaborately decorated; indeed, this copy of Numbers has no decoration at all, although a small blank space was left at the beginning of the text for a decorative initial. Its script, which is legible and certainly serves the purpose of communication adequately, is nonetheless rather unsteady and suggests that it was copied by an inexpert scribe. In his recent study of the production and circulation of glossed books of the Bible, Christopher de Hamel concentrated his attention on manuscripts which can be dated, at least approximately, on the basis of external criteria, especially evidence of early ownership.[2] These books, associated with some of the most important figures of the twelfth century, are often carefully decorated, luxurious manuscripts. It is not a criticism of Dr. de Hamel's pioneering study to note that the evidence from books of this sort needs to be supplemented, and that the study of a broader sample of manuscripts, including more ordinary examples such as MS Lat 334 and MS Richardson 2, will enable us to construct a more complete history of the circulation of the Ordinary Gloss.

This manuscript presents us with yet another example of how one scribe solved the problem of how to arrange the biblical text and the accompanying glosses on the page. Its layout, even more than that of MS Richardson 2 (see cat. no. 33), resembles books ruled according to the "alternate-line" format (see cat. no. 37), with the important exception that the Gloss and the biblical text are still ruled in two separate steps. The three column format, however, with one column of biblical text and two columns of Gloss is no longer the predominant one used. The number of lines and the layout varies from page to page, depending on the length and number of the glosses. On some pages the traditional three column layout is retained. The scribe arranged other pages with the biblical text in a broad column on the inside, with a single column of Gloss on the outside.[3] Pages also occur where the biblical text, copied in the usual large script in long lines, covers the entire page, or is interrupted by small blocks of Gloss.[4] The ruling in this manuscript is so faint that it is often difficult to see, but on most folios the scribe seems to have ignored the prickings and ruled for the text and Gloss as needed, either in hard point or brown crayon.

No bibliography for this manuscript.

NOTES:

[1] Numbers with Glossa Ordinaria; cf. Stegmüller 11784; most of the glosses listed by Stegmüller are included here, but the texts are not identical.

[2] De Hamel, *Glossed Books*, *passim*.; cf. the review by Mo-

nique-Cécile Garand in *Scriptorium* 39 (1985) 322.

[3] For example, f. 11.

[4] For example, ff. 21v-22, and 56.

35. Gilbert de la Porrée, Commentary on the Psalms (77-150)

Italy (Morimondo) s. XII[3/4]   fMS Typ 29

Parchment, ff. i + 161 (foliated 1-160, + 1 unnumbered leaf) + i, 347 x 220 (254-250 x 149) mm. 2 columns, 32 lines. Ruled in lead, with the top 2 or 3, middle 2 or 3 and bottom 2 or 3 horizontal rules full across on some folios; full-length vertical bounding lines, triple between the columns and single on the far inside and outside. Prickings in the three outer margins.

1-18[8] 19[8] (3, f. 147, and 6, f. 150, single) 20[8] (+ 1, following f. 160, with text in a later hand). Horizontal catchwords, very bottom margin in the gutter, quires 17, 18 and 19; quires 1 and 2 signed with roman numerals, flourished on all sides, middle, bottom margin, verso of last leaf.

Written above the top line in a twelfth-century minuscule; 'e' usually written e-cedilla; decorative majuscules.

12- to 4-line red initials with simple pen flourishes, often with highlights in pale yellow wash, at the beginning of the commentary on each psalm; opening words of text following initials in decorative majuscules; biblical lemmata brushed with pale yellow. Purchased by Philip Hofer from J. Martini (Cat. 22, 1931, no. 2); his gift to the library, 1942. Accession record: *41HM-8F. Secundo folio: cognoscat generatio.

THIS COPY OF THE Commentary on the Psalms by Gilbert de la Porrée (d. 1154)[1] has been incorrectly described as a copy of Augustine's *Enarrationes in Psalmos*, at least since the 1930s.[2] This mis-identification is not completely surprising, since large portions of the text are indeed borrowed from Augustine. Gilbert's commentary, which may have been written during Anselm of Laon's lifetime but which seems to have circulated only from about 1130 or later,[3] was an expanded version of the Glossa Ordinaria. Gilbert's text is generally longer and fuller than the Gloss, and structured as a continuous commentary, which could be read without reference to the full biblical text. The commentary on each Psalm begins with brief introductory comments pertaining to the Psalm as a whole, discussing its structure, intent, and similar matters, and then proceeds with a mosaic of extracts from commentaries by patristic and other authors, which provides a continuous commentary on the psalm, verse by verse.

gramum. si patet. Qui autem loquitur
iniqua. idest quilibet maledicus. non
direxit idest non profecit in conspectu ocu
lor meor. et si apuo stultos. non tamen
est apuo me glosus. Jn matutino inter fi
ciebam omis peccatores terre. ut disperderem
de ciuitate dni omis operantes iniquitatem.
Pars tertia. Enumerauit huc usq ipsona
xpi. qo bonis adhesit tantu non malis.
quos tam esse misedic collerit tanquam
in nocte ubi non omnia sunt manifesta.
ubi temptationes. ubi latibula leonum.
idest diaboli. querunt a deo escam sibi.
Vnde dns ait discipulis suis. Sathanas
expetiuit uos uexare sicut triticu. ut
sic manducet. Sicut enim ab homine
triticum non manducetur. nisi primo
contritum ut panis fiat. sic neminem
diabolus manducat. nisi prius tribu
latione contriuerit. Cum aut uenerit
dies ubi omnia manifesta. mali sepa
rabuntur a bonis. & hoc est in matutino
interficiebam omis peccatores terre. Quare
Vt disperderem de ciuitate domini idest
de societate ecclie. omnes operantes inqui
tatem. Vel in psona fidelium. cu dixiss
se uitase malos. conuisus addit. Jn matu
tino idest apparente suggestionis crepu
sculo interficiebam oratione ne crescerent omis
peccatores terre. idest demones qui peccare faci
unt omne carne. ut disperdere de ciuitate dni
que est aia iusti omes operantes iniquitate noe submi
ssione diaboli.

exaudi orationem meam. et clamor meus
ad te ueniat. Titulus. Oratio pauperis
cum anxiaretur. & in conspectu dni effu
dit pecem suam. Psalmus iste penitentia
lium quintus est quartus eor qui dnr
oratio. Xpe qui erat uerbum ds in princi
pio apuo dm. a deo diues qe peu omnia
facta sunt. accipiens formam serui fact
est pauper. et tam non du mea egestate ut
possit dicere. et ueram tanquam panem man
ducaui. Vt igitur tam alto tam una
contemplaret. paupertatem addit paupeti.
nos inse transfigurans ut caput et membra.
in quibus sunt et penitentes. sicut sunt duo
incarne una. ita sunt in uoce una. Vnde
et ysaias ppha dicit se sponsum et sponsa
ita. Sicut sponso alligauit michi mitra.
& sicut sponsam induit me ornamento.
Sponsum dicit se xpe caput. sponsam xpe
menbra. Ergo xpe paup in nobis. cu et xpe
nos caput cum menbris una persona
orat in hoc psalmo p miseriis huius mun
di. in quas xpe peccatum primi parentis
uilto iuditio di deiectus est. Vnde ait.

Plate 23. No. 35. fMS Typ 29, f. 52. 4/5 actual size.

94

The general appearance of this copy of Gilbert's text is similar to many of the manuscripts of commentaries by Augustine, Gregory and others included in the exhibition. A few aids to the reader are incorporated, but the layout is basically very simple. The text is copied continuously in two columns; phrases of the Psalms cited in the course of the discussion are brushed with pale yellow. Abbreviations in the margin indicate when Augustine and Cassiodorus are cited; only the author's name is indicated, and other sources are not identified. Readers, however, seemed to have been dissatisfied with the omission of the full text of the Psalter, possibly because this commentary was so closely associated with the Ordinary Gloss, where the commentary and the biblical text were always copied together. From about 1160, therefore, this text was often copied together with the full text of the Psalms; this layout can be seen in the copy of Gilbert's commentary on the Pauline epistles, also shown here (see cat. no. 36).[4]

Although there is no contemporary ex-libris from Morimondo in this manuscript, it can be ascribed to that Abbey on the basis of its binding, script and decoration.[5] It is almost certainly this manuscript which is listed in Morimondo's library catalogue (see cat. nos. 1 and 10) as number 52, "Psalterium aliud glosatum gisliberti."[6]

BIBLIOGRAPHY: De Ricci, 1695 (= New York, Collection of Philip Hofer, MS 15); Faye and Bond, 254. FURTHER READING: H. C. Van Elswijk, *Gilbert Porreta, sa vie, son oeuvre, sa pensée* (Louvain 1966); N. M. Haring, *The Commentaries on Boethius by Gilbert of Poitiers* (Toronto 1966); de Hamel, *Glossed Books*, 4-7 and 18-20.

NOTES:

[1] There is no modern edition of this text; cf. Stegmüller 2511, summarizing the text and listing some manuscripts.

[2] Cf. the descriptions in De Ricci and Faye and Bond, cited below.

[3] Cf. de Hamel, *Glossed Books*, 5-6, citing the colophon of Oxford, Balliol College MS 36, which states that Gilbert read a draft of the text to Anselm, and noting that the text was used by Geroch of Reichersberg in his commentary on the Psalms written between 1144-48, and a copy of this text was included among the books presented by Prince Henry of France to Clairvaux; de Hamel suggests that Prince Henry's books date from between c. 1135-1149.

[4] The layout of Gilbert's commentaries has been examined in detail in de Hamel, *Glossed Books*, 18-20.

[5] Its script and decoration are similar to those in another Morimondo manuscript, Cambridge, Fitzwilliam Museum, McClean MS 113, Jerome, Commentary on Matthew; see M. R. James, *A Descriptive Catalogue of the McClean Collection of Manuscripts in the Fitzwilliam Museum* (Cambridge 1912) 246 and plate LXXI.

[6] See Leclercq, "Manuscrits cisterciens," 180, no. 52; strictly speaking this copy of Gilbert's Commentary is not a "glossed" Psalter, but the description of the manuscript in this fashion is understandable, since manuscripts of this text were often copied with the full text of the Psalms, as glossed texts. Leclercq, presumably on the basis of the incorrect description printed in De Ricci, interpreted no. 20 in the catalogue, "Item augustini super psalterium," as a reference to this manuscript, which was then in Philip Hofer's collection (*ibid.*, 178).

36. Gilbert de la Porrée, Commentary on the Pauline Epistles
Germany s. XII²   MS Typ 277

Parchment, ff. 168, 304 x 220 mm., ruled space, text and gloss, 226-220 x 156-144 mm. 2 columns: commentary copied in a smaller script in the outer column, 47 lines; ruled in hard point, with double full-length vertical bounding lines; written space of commentary varies depending on ratio of commentary to gloss, (218-216 x 90-80) mm.; biblical text copied in a larger script in the inner column, 26-23 lines; ruled in lead, with single full-length vertical bounding lines; written space of biblical text varies from (226-220 x 75-65) to (215 x 20) mm. Prickings in outer margin correspond to ruling in hard point for the commentary; prickings, top margin, for vertical bounding lines, text and gloss (often ignored by scribe).

1⁸ (-1, 2, 3, 4, 5, 6, 7; stubs remain; cancelled with no loss of text) 2-21⁸ 22⁶ 23⁴ (-2, 3, 4, stubs remain; cancelled with no loss of text). Quire 6, f. 41v, with two horizontal catchwords, very bottom margin, below the text column, for the text, and below the column of gloss, for the gloss. Catchwords for the gloss only remain in quires 7, 9-10, 13-14, 17-18, and 20 (often partially cut away).

Biblical text written in a twelfth-century minuscule approaching gothic, but without letter unions; commentary written in a smaller script with more conservative letter forms. Text and commentary begin above the top ruled line.

F. 1, full-page frontispiece and opening words of biblical text (commentary begins f. 1v), with historiated initial running the full-length of the page in the outer column, of 2 soldiers carrying the body of Paul (?), with God depicted above; initial is outlined in blue and white wash, with three roundels containing bust-length portraits set within a leafy vine, which fills the shaft of the initial, and is entwined around the outline, touched with green, red and blue wash on brushed gold. Thirteen 23- to 8-line painted initials in a similar style at the beginning of the remaining biblical books (initials ff. 110v and 116 are historiated, depicting Paul writing). Three initials, equivalent to 11- to 8-lines of commentary, ff. 2 (beginning of commentary) and 121v (prologue and beginning of commentary), drawn in brown outline, with the shafts filled with blue and red curling leaf-tendrils, and with spirals containing dragons and birds within the initials. Remaining prologues and sections of the commentary begin with red or blue initials, equivalent to 8- to 2-lines of commentary, with simple pen decoration in the other color. Biblical lemmata in commentary underlined in brown ink. Initials in text and commentary messily daubed with red by a later hand; running titles added later. Purchased by Philip Hofer in 1955; his gift to the library, 1 August 1983, "in honor of Rodney G. Dennis." Accession record: *83M-4. Secundo folio: [text] ihesu uocatus; [commentary] *Paulus servus etc.* More scribentium.

GILBERT DE LA PORRÉE's Commentary on the Pauline Epistles was probably written around 1130. Like his earlier Commentary on the Psalms, it was an expanded version of the Ordinary Gloss.¹ In his lifetime both texts seem to have been copied as continuous commentaries (see cat. no. 35). The layout of the manuscript shown here is representative of copies of this text dating after c. 1160.² The scribe copied the commentary first, in a broad column in the outer margin ruled for this purpose. The biblical text was then copied in a much larger script in a narrow column in the inner margin. The problem of aligning the text and the commentary was addressed line by line, a process very evident in this manuscript. For example, on f. 13, in lines 14 and 16, the scribe used a very elongated 'n' in three words to fill out the column of biblical text in a passage with a lengthy commentary. On f. 157, the column of biblical text is very narrow and rather empty, another example of a page where there was a lot of commentary on the passages in

I n primitiua eccłia aliqui ebreoꝝ xpm confitentes: le
gales obseruantias tenendas putabant: ⁊ uihc erꝛore
quosdã etiã qui exgentilibꝫ ueniant ad xpm: sua auctó
ritate inducant. Paulus ᵹ doctoꝛ gentiũ eisdem gen
tibꝫ puidens ne demceps inhc erꝛoꝛem ebreoꝛ auctorita
te trahant ⁊ ut ⁊ suam ademulandũ infide gentiles
puocet carne: qui sic ipse alibi dic̃ e honoꝛ ministe
rij sui. scribit ebreis degřa: ostendens eã p xpm ueru
pontificem fidelibꝫ hoc tpe factam: ⁊ legem omnino
reprobatam. Circa finem uero est moralis instructio:

M ultiphariam ⁊c. Noīm suum
ebreis eoquod illoꝛ legem de
struit odiosum: tacet. ne sup
bis ipse humilis se apłm un
dedignarent appellat. Quidã
autem hanc epłam pauli nonee contendũt
eoquod nonsit eī nomine titulata: sꝫ aut ba
rnabe. aut luce. aut clemtis. Quibꝫ respon
dendũ e qd siᵹptea pauli nonee qꝛ noīm eius
nonht. nec aliculꝝ erit. quia nullꝯ nomme
titulat. Magis ᵹ pauli ee credenda e ᵹtanto
doctrine fulget eloᵹo. Nec sane mirum e si
eloquentioꝛ uidet inᵹꝑo. ı. ebreo. quã ĩ pe
grino. ı. greco quo cetere epłe ꝝ scꝑte sermo
ne: quo ⁊ ipsa p decessũ apłi aluca sensum
⁊ordine eius retinente: fert ee composita.
Gřam ᵹ fidelibꝫ hoc tpe factam p xpm: ipsꝯ
xpꝭti: ⁊ discipuloꝝ eius. ⁊ etiam miracloꝝ que peos facta
sunt. ⁊ donoꝝ sci spꝭ que acceperit attestatione demonstra
turus: sacdotiꝰ ᵹꝫ ⁊ legis uetis translatione rationibꝫ: ⁊ scꝑtu
rum auctoritatibꝫ confirmatuꝛ: ⁊ fidem plurimis creden
tium exemplis commendatuꝛ. xpm gře huꝯ ⁊ auctoꝛe ⁊ teste
ut eī de gřa ista testimonio magis credat: pmo commdat: con
ferens cum oībꝫ pphis ⁊ anglis. ⁊ spetialit̃ moysi pquē lex
data e: ⁊ cum potestate ⁊ natura tũ ⁊ benignitate atᵹ
dignitate his oīb; pferens. Qᵭ de gřa ⁊ legis fine nec exse
nec alia quã pphe pdixãt: nunciare psũpsit. Non exse
quia dꝭ in ipso locutus e. Non alia. qꝛ loquens olim: diebꝫ
istis loquitus e: ad hoc psentis tpis dictione. ı. loquens: cũ
pātꝛ tempoꝛis dictione. ı. olim. conjungit. ⁊ ait. olim locꝝus.
⁊ñe locutus e ᵹ e pātꝛ tempoꝛis. cũ diebꝫ istis qᵭ e psentis. et
ait diebꝫ istis locutus e: ut hac conexione psentis cũ pꝛeterito.
⁊ item pātꝛ cũ psenta. sigcaret̃ te in pphis idem pdixisse dꝭ
ᵹ nouissime infilio nuntiauit: uꝛ te pdixat: tande infilio
nuntiasse. Idem intelligit p hoc quoᵹꝫ ᵹ ait patꝛꝫ ⁊ nob: ı.
eoꝛ filiꝭ. Si eni alij gentꝛ te ⁊ alij ñe loqꝛetur: posꝫ uidi
de dꝛusis locut. Nos aut ⁊ patres: uno uinꝯ di cultu una gentꝭ

ULTI
PHARIA
MULTISQ
MODIS
OLIM DE
ve
LOQVENS
PATRI
BVS
IT

Plate 24. No. 36. MS Typ 277, f. 146. 7/10 actual size.

question. On ff. 38v-39, in contrast, where the commentary was much briefer, the pages are almost entirely covered with the biblical text, which is even written full across the page at the bottom, encroaching on the space usually reserved for the commentary.

Physical details can once again help us to unravel the process of how this book was made. The pages here were first pricked and ruled in hard point for the commentary; the rulings for the biblical text were added later in lead after the scribe copied the commentary, and could judge how much space was needed. The fact that the text and the commentary were copied in two different shades of ink lends further support to the proposal that this book was copied in two stages. As Christopher de Hamel has observed, this procedure is of special interest, because it reverses the usual precedence of the biblical text over the Gloss; in copies of Gilbert de la Porrée's commentary laid-out in this fashion, it is the commentary, rather than the text of the Bible, which determines the appearance of the page.[3]

The manuscript shown here was written in Germany in the second half of the twelfth century. By the fifteenth century it was owned by the House of Augustinian Canons of St. Mary and St. Alexander the Martyr at Halle in Germany.[4] Most twelfth-century manuscripts have been rebound. This manuscript, however, is still bound in its original heavy wooden boards, covered with undecorated leather. This serviceable binding may be compared with the much more decorative binding used on fMS Typ 204 (see cat. no. 32), the only other example of a twelfth-century binding included in the exhibition.

BIBLIOGRAPHY: Faye and Bond, 275.

NOTES:

[1]De Hamel, *Glossed Books*, 5; Stegmüller 2515-2528; there is no modern printed edition of this commentary.

[2]De Hamel, *Glossed Books*, 19-20; cf. plate 6 of Oxford, Bodleian Library MS Lat.th.c.21, with identical layout.

[3]De Hamel, *Glossed Books*, 20.

[4]Fifteenth-century ex-libris note, inside front cover.

37. Sapiential Books with the Ordinary Gloss

Northern France or Flanders s. XIII²/⁴   fMS Lat 6

Parchment, ff. i + 167 + i, 417 x 292 mm., written space, text and gloss, (255-242 x 146-144) mm. 3 columns (two columns of equal size with a wider outer column), 53-49 lines. Ruled in lead, with the top 2 and bottom 2 horizontal rules full across; full-length vertical bounding lines, double in the inner and outer margins; some folios with an additional set of narrow double rules in the outer margin. Layout of each page varies, with one to three columns, depending on the ratio of text to gloss. Text written every other line; the gloss on every line. Prickings in all four margins.

1-4¹⁰ 5⁸ 6¹⁰ 7⁸ 8-10¹⁰ 11⁸ 12-17¹⁰ 18³ (1, f. 165, + conjugate pair). Horizontal catchwords, lower inside margin (some cut away); leaf and quire signatures in very faint lead in most quires, lower right margin, recto, with a letter designating the leaf and a sign, the quire.

Text always copied below the top line; gloss copied below the top line, except when it is continued from the previous page. Text copied in a formal gothic bookhand; gloss in a smaller, less formal, script. One scribe throughout.

Five 9- to 6-line initials (with the exception of 'P,' f. 1, 20-line) in blue and orange, orange, or pink and blue, with touches of yellow on geometrical grounds of polished gold with interior vine scrolls terminating in stylized leaves or animal heads, at the beginning of each book of the Bible (except Ecclesiastes, major initial at chapter 1:2). Similar 6-line initial on a dark pink ground, f. 49v, at the beginning of Ecclesiastes. One 6-line parted red and blue initial with red and gray-green pen flourishes, and two 8- to 4-line blue initials with red pen flourishes used before prologues. Chapters and smaller divisions within the biblical text begin with 2- to 1-line alternating red and blue initials with contrasting pen flourishes, in red or gray-green. Chapter numbers, paragraph marks, and running headlines in red and blue. Tie marks used to indicate the continuation of glosses. Some guide notes for running headlines and chapter numbers. Given by the Massachusetts Historical Society to the Harvard Divinity School, November 24, 1908; transferred to Harvard College Library, May 16, 1912. Secundo folio: [text] [tendicu]las contra; [gloss] In fontem. Qui.

THIS COPY OF THE Sapiential Books with the Ordinary Gloss,[1] was written in Northern France or Flanders in the second quarter of the thirteenth century. The initials are similar to those found in Parisian books of about the same period, but the colors, size, and simplified shapes of the initials, as well as the use of highly polished gold grounds, suggest that the manuscript was not painted in Paris.[2] This handsome, large-format manuscript, which includes the five Sapiential books — Proverbs, Ecclesiastes, the Song of Songs, Wisdom, and Ecclesiasticus — is representative of new developments in the appearance of glossed books. Thirteenth-century Glossed Bibles tend to be larger than twelfth-century copies, and often include more than one book of the Bible.[3]

The format used in this manuscript, however, is not a thirteenth-century innovation, but one which was first used in glossed books around 1160.[4] The leaves were first pricked and ruled in three columns of 53-49 lines. The ruling on each page is basically the same, so the scribe could prepare all his parchment at one time, before he began to copy the text. The scribe then copied the biblical text in a large script on alternate lines, and the Gloss in a smaller script on every line, using this one basic pattern of rulings for both. The number of columns on each page varies from one to three, depending on the ratio of text to gloss. This layout ena-

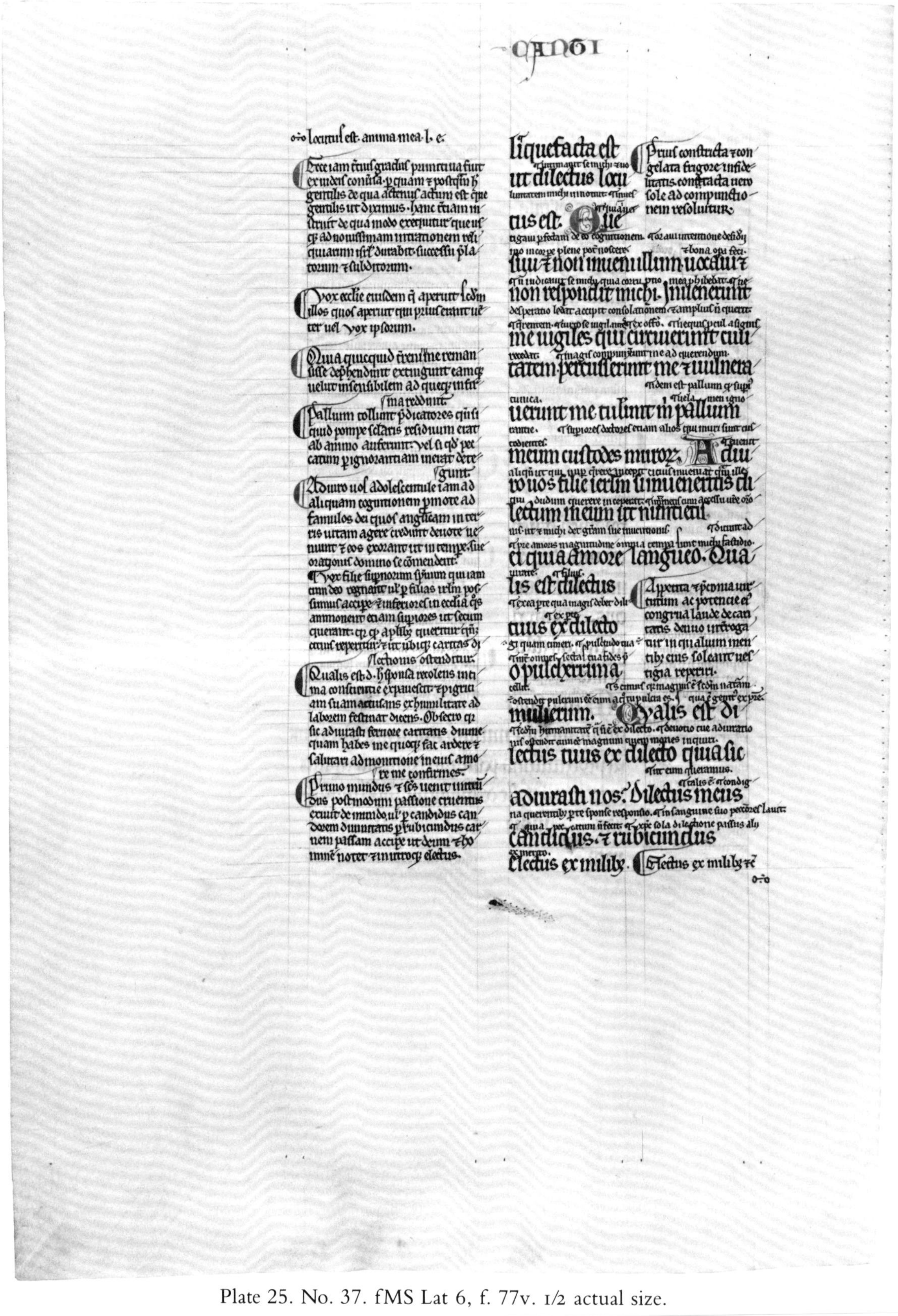

Plate 25. No. 37. fMS Lat 6, f. 77v. 1/2 actual size.

bled the scribe to use virtually the entire page; the blank spaces surrounding the biblical text so evident in a manuscript like MS Typ 260 (see cat. no. 31), with its very conservative layout, provide a good contrast to the closely covered pages in this manuscript. Even in manuscripts like Richardson 2 and Lat 334 (see cat. nos. 33 and 34), where the method used to copy the text and the Gloss is approaching that used here, the use of space is less efficient. Moreover, the scribe of fMS Lat 6, unlike the scribes of these books, did not have to stop and add the rulings for the glosses as he worked.

The use of this "alternate-line" format in manuscripts of glossed books of the Bible is not only an excellent example of skilled book-making, it is also a sign that the content of the Ordinary Gloss was, at least in many cases, regarded as fixed. Variations in the text of the Gloss still occur, but the use of a layout that required so much advanced planning indicates that many copies reproduced their exemplars as closely as possible.

BIBLIOGRAPHY: De Ricci, 976; Harvard College Library, *The Houghton Library 1942-1967; A Selection of Books and Manuscripts in Harvard Collections* (Cambridge, Mass. 1967) 14 (with plate of f. 109v).

NOTES:

[1]Sapiential Books with the Glossa Ordinaria; text of the gloss is generally similar to that described in Stegmüller 11802-11806.

[2]Cf. Robert Branner, *Manuscript Painting in Paris during the Reign of St. Louis: A Study of Styles* (Berkeley 1977) 66-96; the gray-green color used in the pen-scroll initials, and the elaborate majuscules in the script of the text also sug-gest a non-Parisian origin.

[3]Cf. Guy Lobrichon, "Les gloses de la Bible," in *Le Moyen Age et la Bible*, P. Riché and G. Lobrichon, eds., Bible de Tous les Temps 4 (Paris 1984), 101.

[4]On the development of this "alternate line" layout, see de Hamel, *Glossed Books*, 23-27.

38. Peter Comestor, Historia scholastica

Northern France or Flanders s. XIII^{med} MS Lat 226

Parchment, ff. ii + 217 + ii, 264 x 175 (163-160 x 95-92) mm. 2 columns, 43-40 lines. Ruled in lead or brown crayon, with the top 2 and bottom 2 horizontal rules usually full across (in quire 1 the 1st and 3rd rules, top and bottom, are full across on some folios), with additional double horizontal rules, full across, in the top and bottom margins (omitted ff. 187-217, quires 18-20); single full-length vertical bounding lines. Prickings in three outer margins.

1-2^{12} 3^6 (1-4, singletons, + 5/6, conjugate pair) 4-7^{12} 8^{10} 9^7 (all singletons) 10-16^{12} 17^7 (1-3, singletons, with 4/7, ff. 183 and 186, and 5/6, ff. 184-5, two conjugate pairs) 18^{12} 19^{10} 20^{10} (-10 excised, with remains of later text on stub). Horizontal catchwords, lower, inside margin (some cut away); quires 1 and 2 signed in ink in roman numerals, lower, inside margin by the scribe, verso of last leaf; remaining quires quickly signed in roman numerals, lead point or crayon, in later hands; leaf and quire signatures in lead visible in most quires, lower, outer corner, on the recto, with a letter designating the leaf and a mark, the quire; leaves in the quires assembled completely or in part from single leaves (i.e. quires 3, 9, and 17) numbered in early arabics in ink, very bottom, outer corner on the recto.

Written below the top line in a small upright gothic text hand.

Books begin with 6- to 2-line (21-line 'I,' f. 1) parted red and blue initials with red and blue pen flourishes, or with 3-line red or blue initials with pen flourishes in the other color. Chapters begin with alternating red and blue 2-line initials, with pen flourishes of the other color. Red rubrics; majuscules within the text sporadically daubed with red. Some guide letters for the chapter initials in the inner or outer margins. Purchased in 1955 (Susan A. E. Morse Fund). Accession record: *55M-33. Secundo folio: Dixit autem deus.

THE *Historia scholastica* by Peter Comestor (c. 1100-1178) was a phenomenally popular work. Stegmüller's *Repertorium biblicum*, the standard reference work for medieval biblical commentaries, lists over two hundred copies, and this list is not complete.[1] The Comestor's work is a summary of biblical history from Genesis through the Gospels, ending with the Ascension. Most copies of the text include a continuation through the conclusion of the book of Acts, probably written by Peter of Poitiers, who was also the author of the very compressed biblical history found in the manuscript roll exhibited here (see cat. no. 39). In his prologue, Peter Comestor explains that he composed his history in response to the urgent demands of his colleagues, who wanted a convenient compendium of biblical history, which would bring together information scattered throughout the Bible, and supplement information too briefly explained in the Gloss.[2] The success of this work is an indication of how well it answered these demands. By the thirteenth century, and possibly as early as the last decades of the twelfth, it had become a standard school text, and like the Ordinary Gloss on the Bible, it was the subject of lectures. Since the library does not own a twelfth-century copy of this important text, it is represented by this thirteenth-century copy.

An interesting feature of the *Historia scholastica*, which can be seen in MS Lat 226, as well as in many earlier copies, is the way in which the scribe occasionally subdivides a column of text into two narrower columns in order to insert comments on the text. In this manuscript, these comments are copied in the same size script as the text, and are boxed in red. The text of the *Historia scholastica* has not been the subject of a modern critical study. A comparison of a limited number of manuscripts indicates that these additions vary from copy to copy, and suggests that further study of the textual tradition of this work would likely be rewarding.[3]

BIBLIOGRAPHY: Faye and Bond, 242. FURTHER READING: Smalley, *Study of the Bible*, 178-80; S. R. Daly, "Petrus Comestor, Master of Histories," *Speculum* 32 (1957) 62-73; I. Brady, "Peter Manducator and the Oral Teachings of Peter Lombard," *Antonianum* 41 (1966) 454-490.

NOTES:

[1]Stegmüller 6543-6565, and 6785 (continuation by Peter of Poitiers); printed in *PL* 198: 1053-1722. For Peter of Poitiers' contribution, see Philip Samuel Moore, *The Works of Peter of Poitiers, Master in Theology and Chancellor of Paris (1193-1205)*. Publications in Medieval Studies, University of Notre Dame, 1 (Notre Dame, Indiana 1936), 118-122.

[2]*PL* 198:1053-1054.

[3]These glosses or comments in this manuscript are often identical or closely related to those printed at the end of the chapter in the printed edition and marked "additio." Note, however, that this manuscript does not include all of the *additiones* printed in *PL*, and includes some not found in this edition.

39. Peter of Poitiers, Compendium historiae in genealogia christi
Northern France s. XIII[in]   fMS Typ 216

Parchment roll consisting of 6 membranes sewn together, each measuring approximately 70-60 x 38-37 cm. (except the last, 27 x 37 cm.); overall size, 343 x 38-37 cm. Ruled in lead; some prickings remain on the left.

Text runs vertically from top to bottom, on one side only. Written in an upright early gothic book hand, with forked ascenders, and early letter unions.

Thirteen red roundels with pen and ink drawings of important figures mentioned in the text, partly colored in red and blue; some with very pale yellow wash used for shading; tree of consanguinity and candelabra depicted on the first membrane. 3- to 2-line alternately red and blue initials with simple pen flourishes in the other color. Purchased by Philip Hofer from H. P. Kraus in 1954. Deposited by Hofer in the library, January 1, 1967; accession record: *68M-150(70). Hofer bequest, 1984.

Lᴉᴋᴇ Pᴇᴛᴇʀ Cᴏᴍᴇsᴛᴏʀ's *Historia scholastica* (see cat. no. 38), this manuscript roll testifies to the fact that a knowledge of biblical history was considered an essential part of the study of the Bible in the schools by the second half of the twelfth century.[1] Peter Comestor's work provided the student with a convenient exposition of biblical history in one volume. His text, however, was still a demanding one, and certainly rather lengthy. Peter of Poitiers' (c. 1130-1216), *Compendium his-*

toriae in genealogia Christi, attempts to make the student's life even easier.[2] In his prologue, Peter of Poitiers explains that his aim was to help students who were prevented from mastering biblical history because of its length, and because they were too poor to own books.[3] The text he created is the briefest possible summaries of biblical history, presented in the form of a genealogy of Christ, beginning with Adam. The text also includes important biblical figures not directly related to Christ, and concludes with the Apostles and the major political figures of the Apostolic era. All of this material is arranged in a visually arresting manner to aid memorization. The names of the main figures are inscribed in circles which run down the center of the manuscript, with lines showing their relationship; subsidiary people, not directly related to Christ, are grouped off to the side. Pictures of major biblical figures are scattered throughout to further highlight the content of the text.

Peter of Poitiers' text survives in two formats. Many copies are found in traditional codices, usually together with similar works, often the Comestor's *Historia scholastica*. The format of our manuscript, a very early copy of the text, is likely faithful to the author's original intentions. It is possible that rolls such as this one were designed to be hung on the wall in the classroom, and as such, must be the earliest example of visual aids created to make the tasks of teaching and learning easier.[4]

BIBLIOGRAPHY: Faye and Bond, 271; *Harvard Cat.* (1955) p. 14, no. 25 and plate 5 (reproducing upper portion of the second membrane); M. T. Clanchy, *From Memory to Written Record; England 1066-1307* (Cambridge, Mass. 1979) 97 and plate 12 (reproducing detail of the upper portion of the second membrane); William H. Monroe, "A Roll-Manuscript of Peter of Poitiers' Compendium," *The Bulletin of the Cleveland Museum of Art* 65 (1978) 92-107 (discussing Cleveland Museum of Art MS 73.5, an English copy of this text from the early thirteenth century, also in roll-form), especially 95-96, and figure 2b (reproducing most of the second membrane). FURTHER READING: Philip S. Moore, *The Works of Peter of Poitiers: Master in Theology and Chancellor of Paris (1193-1205)*. Publications in Medieval Studies, The University of Notre Dame, 1 (Notre Dame, Indiana 1936).

NOTES:

[1]See especially Smalley, *Study of the Bible*, 83-263.

[2]Stegmüller 6778; Philip S. Moore, *The Works of Peter of Poitiers: Master in Theology and Chancellor of Paris (1193-1205)* Publications in Mediaeval Studies, University of Notre Dame, 1 (Notre Dame, Indiana 1936) 97-117 and appendix III; text of fMS Typ 216 is closest to the version identified by Moore in the appendix as the original, non-interpolated version.

[3]Prologue printed in Moore, *Peter of Poitiers*, 99.

[4]Moore, *Peter of Poitiers*, 108, note 20, citing an entry from Alberic of Trois-Fontaines' Chronicle; while Alberic does not specifically state that the text was used in this way, his wording seems to support the interpretation; cf. Smalley, *Study of the Bible*, 215.

Suggestions for Further Reading

I. GENERAL STUDIES:

Two general volumes containing articles by different scholars on a broad range of topics related to the medieval Bible, including textual history, commentaries and the liturgy, may be mentioned as the indispensable guides to the subject; both include extensive bibliographies: *The Cambridge History of the Bible. Vol. 2, The West from the Fathers to the Reformation,* G. W. H. Lampe, ed. (Cambridge 1969); and *Le Moyen Age et la Bible,* P. Riché and G. Lobrichon, eds., Bible de tous les temps 4 (Paris 1984).

Readers interested in a general introduction to medieval manuscripts may now consult, Robert G. Calkins, *Illuminated Books of the Middle Ages* (Ithaca, New York 1983), which is especially useful for liturgical manuscripts, and Christopher de Hamel, *A History of Illuminated Manuscripts* (Boston 1986), a lively account, which focusses on how the manuscripts were used. A more specialized account is N. R. Ker's exemplary study, *English Manuscripts in the Century after the Norman Conquest* (Oxford 1960).

The best introduction to the great twelfth-century monastic Bibles is Walter Cahn, *Romanesque Bible Illumination* (Ithaca, New York 1983); this study also includes a useful overview of the history of the Bible before the twelfth century, and references to the work of other scholars, especially art historians. The textual history of the Bible in the twelfth century has been the subject of surprisingly little study. The general overviews of the textual history of the Vulgate in the Middle Ages in the *Cambridge History of the Bible,* 2:102-154 and in *Le Moyen Age et la Bible,* 55-93, discuss the twelfth century briefly. H. H. Glunz, *History of the Vulgate in England from Alcuin to Roger Bacon* (Cambridge 1933), should be included here with the warning that his approach to the history of the Vulgate was eccentric, and his work should be consulted with caution.

II. LITURGY:

S. J. P. van Dijk, "The Bible in Liturgical Use," in the *Cambridge History of the Bible,* 220-252, provides a brief sketch of historical developments, and outlines the structure of the Mass and Divine Office. Those interested in more detailed studies may now consult, Richard W. Pfaff, *Medieval Latin Liturgy: A Select Bibliography.* Toronto Medieval Bibliographies 9 (Toronto 1982).

Two of the best brief introductions to medieval liturgical manuscripts are the exhibition catalogues: John Plummer, *Liturgical Manuscripts for the Mass and Divine Office* (New York: Pierpont Morgan Library, 1964), and [S. J. P. van Dijk], *Liturgical Manuscripts and Printed Books; Guide to an Exhibition Held During 1952* (Oxford: Bodleian Library, 1952). Andrew Hughes, *Medieval Manuscripts for Mass and Office: A Guide to their Organization and Terminology* (Toronto 1982), contains a great deal of valuable information; however, beginners should be warned that although this book is presented as an introduction to the subject, it is perhaps best read only after one has a good idea of the basic organization and contents of liturgical manuscripts.

III. BIBLICAL COMMENTARIES:

Our knowledge of the medieval commentary tradition owes more to the work of Beryl Smalley than to any other single scholar; *The Study of the Bible in the Middle Ages* (Oxford, 3rd. rev. ed. 1983) is the classic guide to the subject, which is supplemented by her numerous articles, some of which have been collected in *Studies in Medieval Thought and Learning from Abeland to Wyclif* (London 1981), and in *The Gospels in the Schools c. 1100 — c. 1280* (London 1985). These studies concentrate on the Bible as it was studied in the schools. The monastic side of the tradition is examined in Jean Leclercq, O.S.B., *The Love of Learning and the Desire for God: A Study of Monastic Culture,* Catharine Misrahi, tr. (New York 1961), and in Dom Leclercq's numerous articles, one of which may be mentioned here, "The Renewal of Theology," in *Renaissance and Renewal in the Twelfth Century*, Robert Benson and Giles Constable, with Carol Lanham, eds. (Cambridge, Mass. 1982) 68-87.

IV. THE ORDINARY GLOSS ON THE BIBLE:

The basic textual history of the Glossa Ordinaria is known today largely thanks to the pioneering studies by Beryl Smalley; see her *The Study of the Bible in the Middle Ages*, 46-66, and the articles cited there. Guy Lobrichon, "Une nouveauté: les gloses de la Bible," in *Le Moyen Age et la Bible*, 95-114, is an excellent summary of past research, and includes important new contributions. Christopher de Hamel's, *Glossed Books of the Bible and the Origins of the Paris Booktrade* (Woodbridge, Suffolk 1984) is an innovative study which concentrates on the production of manuscripts of the Glossa Ordinaria, rather than on the history of the text; some of his conclusions deserve closer examination and further research, and his book may usefully be read in conjunction with the reviews by other scholars, including: M-C. Garand in *Scriptorium* 39 (1985) 321-324; M. Gibson in *The Library*, Sixth series, vol. 8 (1986) 166-169; and Walter Cahn in *Speculum* 62 (1987) 408-409.

A Preliminary Checklist of Other Twelfth-Century Manuscripts in the Houghton Library

pfMS Judaica 31

Two charters of Willelmus, son of Castanea of Basingstoke granting land; Winchester, ca. 1170. 2ff. Presented by Lee M. Friedman in 1957. Faye and Bond, 236.

MS Lat 27

Vitae SS. Anselmi, Maioli, Odilonis, Odonis et Hugonis; Holme Cultram, s.XII⁴ᐟ⁴. 84ff. Presented by Dr. Winslow Lewis in 1861. De Ricci, 978; Harvard Cat. (1955), no. 17.

bMS Lat 99

see bMS Lat 229 (2).

bMS Lat 100 (1)

Hymnal; Germany, s.XII. 8ff. Removed from the binding of an early book. De Ricci 983.

bMS Lat 100 (2-3)

2 unidentified fragments from early bindings; s.XII. 2ff and 1f.

MS Lat 127

Boethius. De consolatione philosophiae; Germany, s.XII/XIII. 78ff. Purchased from Tregaskis with the Constantius fund in 1919. De Ricci, 986.

fMS Lat 130

Missal (fragment in Beneventan script); Italy, s.XII². 1f. Presented by Walter Ashburner in 1927. De Ricci, 986.

fMS Lat 157

Liturgical fragment (in Beneventan script); Italy, s.XII². 1f. Purchased from Erik von Scherling with the Treat fund in 1937. Faye and Bond, 237.

MS Lat 184

Homiliary and Office Lectionary; Germany, s.XII. 101ff. Assembled in the fifteenth century from three twelfth-century MSS. Purchased from Otto H. Ranschburg with the Treat fund in 1941. Faye and Bond, 239.

MS Lat 198

Ganymed and Helen; Northern France, s.XII/XIII. roll 56cm. Purchased from E. Weil with the Bemis fund in 1950. Faye and Bond, 240.

bMS Lat 229 (1)

Leonardi vita et miracula (fragment); Italy, s.XII. 1f. (removed from a binding in two pieces). Presented by Ward M. Canaday in 1963.

bMS Lat 229 (2)

Lectionary (fragment), Germany, s.XII. 1f. Removed from a binding. De Ricci, 983 (as MS Lat 99).

MS Lat 292

Commentary on Matthew 4.3 to 5.22; Northern France, XIIᵉˣ. 10ff. Possibly a school commentary. No source or date of acquisition.

MS Lat 300

Anthology of Latin poems; France, s.XII. 11ff. Includes Biblical Epigrams of Hildebertus Turonensis. Purchased from Nicolaus Rauch with the Lincoln fund in 1965.

MS Lat 336

Persius. Satires with commentary; France, s.XII¹ᐟ⁴. 42ff. Purchased at a Sotheby sale (21 November 1972) with the Friends of the Harvard College Library fund.

MS Lat 360 (1)

Missal (fragment); France s.XII¹. 1f. Prayers for the feast of St. Clemens. Presented by W. H. Bond in honor of Arthur A. Houghton, Jr. in 1986.

MS Lat 360 (2)

Antiphonary (fragment); France, s.XII. 2f. Songs for the feast of St. Remigius. Presented by W. H. Bond in honor of Arthur A. Houghton, Jr. in 1986.

MS Richardson 20

Priscian. Grammatica; Italy, s.XII. 212ff. Presented by William King Richardson in 1951. De Ricci, 960.

MS Richardson 26

Augustine. De pastoribus et de ovibus, De baptismo contra donatistas, etc.; Bury St. Edmunds, s.XII²/⁴. 148ff. Original binding. Presented by William King Richardson in 1951. Faye and Bond, 246; Harvard Cat. (1955), no. 9.

MS Typ 194

Rufinus. Historia monachorum, etc.; Llanthony, Monmouth (?), s.XII^med-3/4. 159ff. Early binding. Purchased from B. Halliday in 1953; bequeathed by Philip Hofer in 1984. Faye and Bond, 269. Harvard Cat. (1955), no. 8.

MS Typ 209

Processional; England, ca. 1200. 10ff. Original binding. Purchased from H. P. Kraus in 1954; bequeathed by Philip Hofer in 1984. Faye and Bond, 270; Harvard Cat. (1955), no. 28.

MS Typ 284.1

see pfMS Typ 704 (4).

MS Typ 290

Augustine. De Trinitate. Southern France, s.XII^ex. 115ff. Bequeathed by Philip Hofer in 1984.

MS Typ 318

Gregory. Liber regule pastoralis. France, s.XI. 141ff. Last leaf has a noted hymn, "Alma redemptoris mater," from Eastern France, s.XII. Bequeathed by Philip Hofer in 1984.

pfMS Typ 405

A box of single leaves including:

Lectionary (fragment); Italy, s.XII. 1f. Contains readings from Luke XIV & XV and Matthew V. Presented by William Bentinck-Smith in 1965.

Vitae Sanctorum (?, fragment); Italy, s.XII^med. 1f. Purchased from G. Goodspeed and presented by Philip Hofer in 1976.

Augustine. Epistolae; Italy, s.XII². 1f. Pre-

sented in 1955 by Dr. E. B. Krumbhaar. De Ricci, 1993; Faye and Bond, 276.

Sermon (unidentified fragment); Italy, s.XII². 1f. Presented in 1955 by E. B. Krumbhaar. De Ricci, 1993; Faye and Bond, 276.

MS Typ 423

Isidore, Quaestiones de veteri testamento; France, s.XII. 171ff. Purchased from Day's Ltd. and presented by Philip Hofer in 1956. Faye and Bond, 277.

fMS Typ 424

Ambrose. De Abraham, De Isaac et anima, etc. Hautecombe, s.XII. 187ff. Purchased from Arthur Rau and presented by Philip Hofer in 1956. Faye and Bond, 277.

MS Typ 584

Septenarium pictum. Northern France, s.XII/ XIII. 1f. Purchased from B. M. Rosenthal and presented by Mr. & Mrs. James H. Case, 3rd in 1971.

MS Typ 700

Bible (fragment in Beneventan script): Paul, First Corinthians VII; Italy, s.XII. 1f. Purchased from B. M. Rosenthal in 1964; bequeathed by Philip Hofer in 1984.

fMS Typ 701

Missal (fragment in Beneventan script): Italy, s.XII. 1f. Purchased from B. M. Rosenthal in 1972; bequeathed by Philip Hofer in 1984.

pfMS Typ 704

A box of single leaves:

1. Drawing of Christ with a diagram of consanguinity; France, s.XII^ex/XIII^in. 1f. Purchased from B. M. Rosenthal in 1955; bequeathed by Philip Hofer in 1984.

2. Missal (fragment); Italy, s.XII¹. 1f. Purchased from F. Roux Devillas in 1959; bequeathed by Philip Hofer in 1984.

3. Bible (fragment: Mark XIV. 26-); England (?) s.XII¹. 1f. Bequeathed by Philip Hofer in 1984.

4. Gregory. Homilia XXXVIII (fragment); France, s.XII. 1f. Purchased from W. Schatzki in 1960; bequeathed by Philip Hofer in 1984. Faye and Bond, 275. Formerly pfMS Typ 284.1.

5. Noted Missal (fragment); Milchstätt (?), s.XII. 1f. Purchased from B. M. Rosenthal in 1955; bequeathed by Philip Hofer in 1984. See also no. (6) in this series.

6. Noted Missal (fragment); Milchstätt (?), s.XII. 1f. Purchased from B. M. Rosenthal in 1955; bequeathed by Philip Hofer in 1984. See also no. (5) in this series.

7. Breviary (fragment); Spain — Southern France, s.XII. 1f. Bequeathed by Philip Hofer in 1984.

8. Antiphonary (fragment); Southern France, s.XII. 2ff. Purchased from B. M. Rosenthal in 1964; bequeathed by Philip Hofer in 1984.

9. Commentary on the Psalms (unidentified fragment); Italy (?), s.XII². 1f. Purchased from Eisemann in 1957; bequeathed by Philip Hofer in 1984.

10. Pontifical (fragment); Italy (?), s.XII/XIII. 2ff. Purchased from B. M. Rosenthal; bequeathed by Philip Hofer in 1984.

11. Vita S. Blasii (fragment); Italy, s.XII. 1f. Purchased from B. M. Rosenthal in 1958; bequeathed by Philip Hofer in 1984.

12. Homiliary (fragment); Germany, s.XII^{ex}. 1f. Purchased from Maggs in 1963, bequeathed by Philip Hofer in 1984.

13. Evangeliary (fragment); Italy, s.XII. 1f. Bequeathed by Philip Hofer in 1984.

14. Noted Responsorial (fragment); Italy, s.XII¹. 1f. Purchased from H. P. Kraus (n.d.); bequeathed by Philip Hofer in 1984.

15. Epistolary (fragment); Italy, s.XII. 2ff. Purchased from B. M. Rosenthal in 1959; bequeathed by Philip Hofer in 1984.

16. Lectionary (fragment); Italy, s.XII¹. 1f. Purchased from Mrs. O. F. Ege in 1956; bequeathed by Philip Hofer in 1984.

17. Lectionary (fragment); Austria (?), s.XII. 1f. Part of a leaf with an initial depicting Maria Magdalena. Purchased from l'Art Ancien in 1963; bequeathed by Philip Hofer in 1984.

18. Gregory. Sermo de mortalitate, etc. (fragment); Italy, s.XII. 1f. Bequeathed by Philip Hofer in 1984.

fMS Typ 705

Bede. Homilia XXII. Anchin, s.XII. 1f. Part of a leaf with two figure drawings in the margins. Purchased from H. P. Kraus in 1962; bequeathed by Philip Hofer in 1984.

Concordance of Numbers

MANUSCRIPT NUMBER	CATALOGUE NUMBER
fMS Lat 6	no. 37, pl. 25
MS Lat 44	no. 30
MS Lat 150	no. 17
MS Lat 158	no. 16
MS Lat 167	no. 20, pl. 13
fMS Lat 168	no. 27
MS Lat 185	no. 28, pl. 19
MS Lat 213	no. 23
MS Lat 226	no. 38
MS Lat 264	no. 6
MS Lat 282	no. 14, pl. 9
MS Lat 334	no. 34
MS Riant 20	no. 5, pl. 4
MS Riant 36	no. 29
MS Richardson 2	no. 33, pl. 22
MS Richardson 14	no. 24, pl. 16
MS Richardson 25	no. 22, pl. 15
MS Richardson 27	no. 18, pl. 11
MS Typ 3	no. 4, pl. 3
fMS Typ 29	no. 35, pl. 23
fMS Typ 119	no. 3
fMS Typ 138	no. 9
fMS Typ 200	no. 25, pl. 17
fMS Typ 202	no. 26, pl. 18
fMS Typ 204	no. 32, pl. 21
MS Typ 205	no. 21, pl. 14
fMS Typ 210	no. 8, pl. 5
fMS Typ 216	no. 39
fMS Typ 223	nos. 1 and 10, pl. 1 and 6
MS Typ 260	no. 31, pl. 20
MS Typ 277	no. 36, pl. 24
fMS Typ 291	no. 12, pl. 8
fMS Typ 315	no. 2, pl. 2
MS Typ 413	no. 7
fMS Typ 441	no. 13
MS Typ 444	no. 11, pl. 7
fMS Typ 702	no. 19, pl. 12
fMS Typ 703	no. 15, pl. 10

Index

Items included in the catalogue are listed by manuscript number and catalogue number; manuscripts in the checklist are listed by manuscript number only. Manuscripts in other collections are listed under "Manuscripts cited," alphabetically by location.

Gladbach, Benedictine Monastery of St. Vitus. fMS Typ 202 (no. 26).

Gospel Harmony, with the preface by Victor of Capua. MS Richardson 25 (no. 22).

Gospel Lectionary for the Mass, see Evangeliary.

Gregory the Great, *Moralia in Job*. fMS Typ 702, books 26-35 (no. 19); MS Lat 167, books 23-29 (no. 20); see also no. 21.

— *Homilia XXXVIII*. pfMS Typ 704(4), fragment (checklist).

— *Liber regule pastoralis*. MS Typ 318 (checklist).

— *Sermo de mortalitate*. pfMS Typ 704(18), fragment (checklist).

Halle, Germany, House of Augustinian Canons of St. Mary and St. Alexander the Martyr. MS Typ 277 (no. 36).

Hautecombe, Cistercian Monastery of St. Mary. fMS Typ 424 (checklist).

Hildebert of Lavardin, Poems. MS Riant 36 (no. 29).

Hildebertus Turonensis, Biblical Epigrams. MS Lat 300 (checklist).

Holme Cultram. Cistercian Abbey of St. Mary. MS Lat 27 (checklist).

Homiliary. fMS Typ 441, fragment (no. 13); MS Lat 184 (checklist); pfMS Typ 704(12), fragment (checklist).

Hours of the Virgin. MS Lat 282, fragment (no. 14).

Hugh of St. Victor, *Sententiae*. MS Lat 185 (no. 28).

Hugo, Abbot of Cluny, *Life of*. MS Lat 27 (checklist).

Hymn, "Alma redemptoris mater." MS Typ 318 (checklist).

Hymnal. bMS Lat 100(1) (checklist); see also Office Hymnal.

Isidore, *Quaestiones de veteri testamento*. MS Typ 423 (checklist).

Ivo of Chartres, *Sermons*. MS Riant 36, selections from (no. 29).

Jerome, *Commentary on Daniel*. fMS Lat 168 (no. 27).

— *Letters*. MS Riant 36 (no. 29).

Latin poems, Anthology of. MS Lat 300 (checklist).

Lectionary. bMS Lat 229(2), fragment (checklist); pfMS Typ 405, fragment (checklist); pfMS Typ 704(16), fragment (checklist); pfMS Typ

704(17), fragment (checklist); see also Evangeliary and Office Lectionary.

Leonardi vita et miracula. bMS Lat 229(1), fragment (checklist).

Liturgical fragment. fMS Lat 157 (checklist).

Llanthony, Monmouthshire, Augustine Priory of St John the Baptist. MS Typ 194 (introduction and checklist).

Maiolus, Abbot of Cluny, *Life of*. MS Lat 27 (checklist).

MANUSCRIPTS CITED:

Baltimore. Walters Art Gallery.
    MS W. 778 (nos. 24-25, note 7).
Berlin. Staatsbibliothek.
    MS theol. lat. 379 (nos. 24-25).
Cambridge. Fitzwilliam Museum.
    McClean MS 8 (nos. 1 and 10).
    McClean MS 29 (no. 1).
    McClean MS 113 (nos. 1 and 35).
    McClean MSS 116-117 (no. 1 and nos. 19-20, note 5).
Cambridge. Trinity College.
    MS B.4.30 (no. 4).
Cleveland. Museum of Art.
    MS 73.5 (no. 39).
Côme. Seminario Maggiore.
    MSS (IX-5) and (X-6) (no. 1).
Florence. Biblioteca Laurenziana.
    MS Plut. 14.1 (no. 12, note 2).
    MS Plut. 16.41 (no. 12, note 2).
    MS Plut. 17.39 (no. 12, note 2).
Los Angeles. J. Paul Getty Museum.
    MS Ludwig I. 10 (no. 3).
London. British Museum.
    Additional MS 38687 (nos. 24-25, note 7).
London. University College.
    MS Lat 7 (nos. 24-25, note 7).
Lugano. Collection of E. Rosenthal.
    Leaf from a Bible, with the beginning of Ruth (no. 3).
Montpellier. Bibliothèque de l'École de Medecine.
    MS 12 (nos. 24-25).
New Haven. Yale University. Beinecke Library.
    MS 349 (nos. 24-25, note 12).
Oxford. Bodleian Library.
    Broxbourne Library, Glossed John (no. 32).

MS Canon. Pat. Lat. 214 (no. 10).
MS Lat.th.c.21 (no. 36, note 2).
Paris. Bibliothèque Nationale.
MS lat. 654 (no. 9).
MS lat. 797 (no. 9).
MS lat. 8823 (no. 2 and nos. 24-25).
Philadelphia. Museum of Art.
MS 46-65-1 (no. 3).
Princeton, New Jersey. Princeton University Library.
MS 6 (no. 8).
Trier. Dombibliothek.
MS 133 (no. 11).
Troyes. Bibliothèque municipale.
MS 27 (nos. 24-25).
Tuxedo Park, New York. Collection of Grenville Kane.
MS 1 (no. 8).
Vatican City. Biblioteca Apostolica Vaticana.
MS Barberini 3229 (no. 1 and nos. 19-20, note 3).
MS Vat. lat. 10680 (no. 8).
Washington, D. C. National Gallery of Art.
Rosenwald Collection, MSS 6 and 7 (no. 3).
Present Location Unknown.
J. R. Abbey Collection. MS 7369 (nos. 1 and 8).
Hachette Collection, now in a German private Collection, listed in sales cat. of Alan G. Thomas, no. 4 (1958) p. 2, lot 3 (no. 2).
Phillipps MS 3274 (nos. 24-25, note 7).
Sotheby's, London, 5 December 1978, lot 8 (no. 2).

———

Missal. MS Typ 413, fragments (no. 7); fMS Lat 130, fragment (checklist); MS Lat 360(1), fragment (checklist); fMS Typ 701, fragment (checklist); pfMS Typ 704(2), fragment (checklist); pfMS Typ 704(5 and 6), fragments (checklist).
Morimondo, Italy, Cistercian monastery of St. Mary. fMS Typ 223 (nos. 1 and 10); fMS Typ 210 (no. 8, see also no. 1); fMS Typ 702 (no. 19, see also no. 1); MS Richardson 2 (no. 33, see also no. 1); fMS Typ 29 (no. 35, see also no. 1).
Morimondo library catalogue. fMS Typ 223 (no. 1).

Oberwesel, Benedictine Convent of All Saints. MS Typ 444 (no. 11).
Odilo, Abbot of Cluny, *Life of*. MS Lat 27 (checklist).
Odo, Abbot of Cluny, *Life of*. MS Lat 27 (checklist).
Office Book. MS Lat 282 (no. 14); see also Breviary and Office Lectionary.
Office Hymnal for Franciscan Use. MS Lat 282 (no. 14).
Office Lectionary. fMS Typ 223 (nos. 1 and 10, see also nos. 8 and 11); MS Typ 444 (no. 11); MS Lat 184 (checklist); see also Homiliary and Sermologus.
Office of the Dead. MS Lat 282, fragment (no. 14).
Ordinary Gloss on the Bible. see Introduction to section IV; Psalms with the Ordinary Gloss, MS Typ 260 (no. 31, see also no. 37); Leviticus with the Ordinary Gloss, fMS Typ 204 (no. 32); Gospel of John with the Ordinary Gloss, MS Richardson 2 (no. 33, see also nos. 34 and 37); Numbers with the Ordinary Gloss, MS Lat 334 (no. 34, see also no. 37); Sapiential Books with the Ordinary Gloss, fMS Lat 6 (no. 37).
Paterius, *Liber Testimoniorum*. see no. 21.
Patristic extracts. MS Lat 185 (no. 28); MS Riant 36 (no. 29, see also no. 27).
Persius, *Satires*, with commentary. MS Lat 336 (checklist).
Peter the Chanter. see Introduction to section IV.
Peter Comestor, *Historia scholastica*. MS Lat 226 (no. 38, see also no. 39).
Peter Comestor. see Introduction to section IV.
Peter Lombard. see Introduction to section IV, and no. 31.
Peter of Poitiers, *Compendium historiae in genealogia christi*. fMS Typ 216 (no. 39, see also no. 38).
Pontifical. pfMS Typ 704(10), fragment (checklist).
Pontigny. Cistercian monastery of St. Mary. fMS Typ 315 (no. 2, see also nos. 24-25); MS Richardson 14 (no. 24, see also nos. 2 and 23); fMS Typ 200 (no. 25, see also nos. 2 and 23).
Priscian, *Institutiones grammaticae*. MS Lat 44 (no. 30); MS Richardson 20 (checklist).
Processional. MS Typ 209 (checklist).
Psalter. MS Lat 282 (no. 14).

Rabanus Maurus, *Commentary on Jeremiah and Lamentations.* fMS Typ 200 (no. 25, see also nos. 2, 23 and 26).

Ralph of Laon. see Introduction to section IV.

Reformed script. no. 12, note 3, citing fMS Typ 138 (no. 9), fMS Typ 441 (no. 13), fMS Lat 168 (no. 27), and MS Typ 260 (no. 31).

Remigius of Auxerre, *On the Celebration of the Mass.* MS Lat 158 (no. 16).

Responsorial. pfMS Typ 704(14), fragment (checklist).

Rufinus, *Historia monachorum.* MS Typ 194 (checklist).

Sacramentary. MS Typ 413, incorrectly identified as (no. 7).

Sententiae, monastic. MS Lat 185 (no. 28, also see no. 29); MS Riant 36 (no. 29).

Septenarium pictum. MS Typ 584 (checklist).

Sermologus. fMS Typ 291, fragments (no. 12, see also no. 13).

Sermon, unidentified fragment. pfMS Typ 405 (checklist).

Stephen Langton. see Introduction to section IV.

Taitian, *Diatessaron.* see no. 22.

Unidentified fragments. bMS Lat 100(2-3) (checklist).

Victor of Capua, preface to Gospel Harmony. MS Richardson 25 (no. 22).

Vitae SS. Anselmi, Maioli, Odilonis, Odonis et Hugonis. MS Lat 27 (checklist).

Vitae sanctorum. pfMS Typ 405, fragment (checklist).

Weissenau, House of Premonstratensian Canons. MS Lat 213 (no. 23).

Willelmus, son of Castanea of Basingstoke, two charters. pfMS Judaica 31 (checklist).

Zachary of Besançon (also known as Zacharias Chrysopolitanus). see no. 22.